DESSERT *First*

We are grateful for the organizations and individuals who contributed to our book's sweet taste of success with the following ingredients:

- gallons of generous support from Ohio Restaurant Association chefs, owners, and operators, who shared unique recipes for this book

- stirred in with White Castle Management Company and their team members, who initiated the vision and then helped us reach across the state of Ohio to gather the recipes included

- served around Ohio because of Bob Evans Farms Inc. and especially Larry Corbin, whose generosity will ensure that the message of this book will be communicated

- decorated by our ProStart® students and faculty, who shared their stories and their tasty favorites

- baked until done by Bradie Rice, ORA, and Melissa Jacobs, OHEF, with patience and support, as well as a critical eye for the finished product

- and the icing is each and every one of you. It is because of the part you have played in this project that OHEF can continue its efforts to support some of the best and brightest of Ohio's youth on their life's journey.

DESSERT
First

OHIO HOSPITALITY EDUCATIONAL FOUNDATION

Published by the Ohio Hospitality Educational Foundation

Copyright © 2005 by
Ohio Hospitality Educational Foundation
1525 Bethel Road, Suite 301
Columbus, Ohio 43220
www.ohef.com

For more information, contact
Betty Kaye, OHEF State Director
Telephone: 614-442-9374   Fax: 614-442-9372
Email: bkaye@ohef.com

This cookbook is a collection of recipes, which are not necessarily original.

All rights reserved. No part of this publication may be reproduced in any form or by any means, electronic or mechanical, including photocopy and information storage and retrieval systems, without permission in writing from the publisher.

ISBN: 0-9759269-0-X
Library of Congress Number: 2004097722

Edited, Designed, and Manufactured by Favorite Recipes® Press
An Imprint of

P.O. Box 305142, Nashville, Tennessee 37230
800-358-0560

Art Director: Steve Newman
Designer: Sheri Ferguson
Project Manager: Jane Hinshaw
Project Editor: Debbie Van Mol
Photography: Copyright © StockFood

Manufactured in the United States of America
First Printing 2005
10,000 copies

OHEF

Ohio Hospitality Educational Foundation

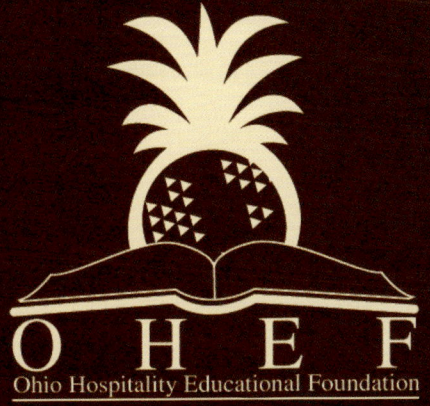

The Ohio Hospitality Educational Foundation (OHEF) is a 501 (c) 3 nonprofit organization dedicated to helping Ohio's high school students learn about the diverse opportunities available in the food service industry.

OHEF's mission is to prepare high school students for top-wage, high-skill careers in the hospitality industry through the implementation of the National Restaurant Association Educational Foundation's (NRAEF) ProStart® program. A curriculum designed and developed for high school juniors and seniors, ProStart® provides teachers and students with a combination of classroom learning and real experience in a mentored worksite. A National Certificate of Achievement, college credits, and scholarship opportunities are also part of the program.

National Restaurant Association
EDUCATIONAL FOUNDATION

ProStart®
School-to-Career Program
National Restaurant Association
Educational Foundation

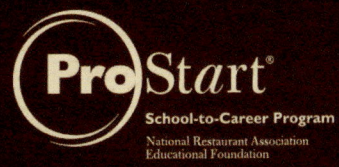

A *Message* from the Ohio Restaurant Association

In October 2000 when the ORA created the Ohio Hospitality Educational Foundation, we were excited to bring to our state a nationally recognized program, ProStart®, that gives high school juniors and seniors a taste for success by providing them with real skills and real experiences. Many of us have had the privilege of assisting hard-working educators and mentoring talented young people while supporting this unique school-to-career initiative.

This recipe book contains recipes from ProStart® students and teachers, along with some interesting tidbits about their accomplishments and future goals. In addition, we've included recipes from ORA members, credentialed chefs, owner/operators, and other good cooks that are sure to broaden your dessert options.

Proceeds from the sale of each cookbook go to the Ohio Hospitality Educational Foundation. By supporting the foundation, you will help us educate, train, and mentor Ohio's ProStart® students and help them move forward to rewarding career opportunities and a secure future.

We hope you enjoy these recipes, and we thank you for supporting the Ohio Hospitality Educational Foundation.

With our gratitude,

Rick Cassara
84th Chairman
Ohio Restaurant Association

Contents

Cakes 8

Cheesecakes 38

Custards · Mousses · Puddings 50

Fruit Desserts 72

Pies · Tarts · Pastries 90

Contributors 118

Index 122

Order Information 127

Chocolate Cake with Chocolate Ganache

Coca-Cola Cake

Chocolate Melt Cakes

Flourless Cakes

Deep Dark Chocolate Cake

Chocolate Espresso Cake

German Chocolate Cake

Red Velvet Cake

Texas Sheet Cake

Warm Chocolate Cake

Chocolate Cream Cheese Cake

Chocolate Malt Brownies

Berry Delicious Cake with White Chocolate Buttercream Icing

Carrot Cakes with White Chocolate Frosting

Cinnamon-Grilled Pound Cake

Lemon Sponge with Raspberry Cream Filling

Mandarin Orange Cake

Pumpkin Roll

Piña Colada Party Cakes with Pineapple Frosting

Torte

Chocolate Cake
Serves 16

CAKE
1 1/2 cups cake flour
1/2 cup baking cocoa
1 teaspoon baking powder
1/4 teaspoon baking soda
1 cup (2 sticks) unsalted butter, softened
1 1/3 cups sugar
2 eggs
1 cup sour cream

BUTTERCREAM ICING AND ASSEMBLY
2 cups sugar
9 ounces water
12 ounces egg whites
3 pounds (12 sticks) unsalted butter, sliced
Chocolate Ganache (page 11)
Rolled Fondant (page 11)
Gumpaste Flowers (page 11)

For the cake, preheat the oven to 350 degrees. Sift the flour, baking cocoa, baking powder and baking soda onto baking parchment. Combine the butter and sugar in a mixing bowl and beat at medium speed until creamy, scraping the bowl occasionally. Beat in the eggs 1 at a time. Add 1/2 of the flour mixture and beat at low speed until blended; scrape the bowl. Beat in the sour cream until smooth. Add the remaining flour mixture and beat until blended. Spoon the batter into 2 greased and floured 10-inch cake pans and bake for 40 to 45 minutes or until the layers test done.

For the icing, bring the sugar and water to a boil in a saucepan, stirring occasionally. Boil until the mixture registers 230 degrees on a candy thermometer. Beat the egg whites in a heatproof mixing bowl until light. Add the hot syrup mixture to the egg whites and beat with a mixer fitted with a paddle attachment until combined. Add the butter gradually, mixing well after each addition.

To assemble, cut off the domed top of each layer; place 1 layer on a serving plate. Spread with a thin layer of Chocolate Ganache. Let stand until set. Spread with Buttercream Icing. Add the second cake layer and spread the top and side of the cake with the icing. Roll 2/3 of the Rolled Fondant large enough to fit over the cake on a surface lightly dusted with cornstarch. Place on the cake and press to fit. Roll the remaining fondant and shape into a swag. Press onto the cake. Arrange the Gumpaste Flowers on the cake, securing with Buttercream Icing.

Whitney Bray
Northeast Career Center '04
Columbus, Ohio

Whitney Bray was a ProStart® student at Northeast Career Center. As an intern with Cameron Mitchell Restaurants' Ocean Club, Whitney is also grateful to her instructor, Pegeen Cleary, and the ProStart® program for expanding her knowledge of the career path available. Pastry arts is her passion, earning her a three-star rating in both her junior and senior years at the Family Career and Community Leaders of America competition at both the regional and state levels. She finished number one in the state in 2004. She is also a recipient of the Ian Van Hyde Memorial Scholarship from the Central Ohio Restaurant Association. Whitney would like to be an executive pastry chef and eventually own her own business.

Chocolate Ganache
Makes enough for 1 cake

1/2 cup heavy cream
8 ounces bittersweet chocolate, chopped or grated

Bring the heavy cream to a boil in a saucepan and remove from the heat. Add the chocolate and stir until smooth.

Rolled Fondant
Makes enough for 1 cake

1 tablespoon gelatin
1/4 cup water
8 cups confectioners' sugar

1/2 cup corn syrup
2 tablespoons vegetable oil
Cornstarch

Sprinkle the gelatin over the water in a saucepan and let stand for about 5 minutes to soften. Heat over low heat until the gelatin dissolves. Combine the confectioners' sugar, corn syrup and oil in a mixing bowl and stir in the gelatin mixture. Beat at low speed until blended, scraping the bowl occasionally. Chill, covered, for a few minutes or until firm.

Gumpaste Flowers
Makes enough for 1 cake

4 egg whites
4 teaspoons shortening

1/4 cup (level) tyclose
8 ounces confectioners' sugar

Beat the egg whites in a mixing bowl with a mixer fitted with a paddle attachment. Add the shortening and beat until combined. Mix the tyclose and confectioners' sugar in a bowl and add to the egg white mixture, beating until blended. Wrap in plastic wrap and chill until firm. Shape into flowers and leaves.

Coca-Cola Cake
Serves 15

2 cups flour
1 3/4 cups sugar
3 tablespoons baking cocoa
1 teaspoon baking soda
1 cup (2 sticks) butter, softened
1/2 cup milk
2 eggs
1 teaspoon vanilla extract
1 cup Coca-Cola
Coca-Cola Frosting (page 13)

Preheat the oven to 350 degrees. Combine the flour, sugar, baking cocoa and baking soda in a mixing bowl and mix well. Add the butter, milk, eggs and vanilla to the flour mixture and beat at low speed for 1 minute; scrape the bowl. Add the Coca-Cola and beat until blended, scraping the bowl occasionally.

Spoon the batter into a 9×13-inch cake pan and bake for 40 to 45 minutes or until the edges pull from the sides of the pan. Cool in the pan on a wire rack. Spread with the Coca-Cola Frosting.

Jack Edwards, CEC
Adams Mark Hotel
Columbus, Ohio

Coca-Cola Frosting
Makes 3 to 4 cups

4 cups confectioners' sugar
1/2 cup (1 stick) butter, softened
1/3 cup Coca-Cola
3 tablespoons baking cocoa
1 cup pecans, toasted and chopped

Combine the confectioners' sugar, butter, Coca-Cola and baking cocoa in a mixing bowl. Beat until smooth and of a spreading consistency, scraping the bowl occasionally. Stir in the pecans.

Chocolate Melt Cakes
Serves 12

Butter for coating
14 ounces semisweet chocolate, chopped
1 1/4 cups (2 1/2 sticks) butter
1 tablespoon baking cocoa
6 eggs
6 egg yolks
3 tablespoons chocolate liqueur
3 cups confectioners' sugar, sifted
1 cup flour
Confectioners' sugar to taste

Preheat the oven to 425 degrees. Coat twelve 1/2-cup soufflé baking dishes with butter. Combine the chocolate, 1 1/4 cups butter and the baking cocoa in a saucepan. Cook over low heat until smooth, stirring constantly. Cool slightly.

Whisk the eggs and egg yolks in a bowl until blended. Whisk in the liqueur. Add 3 cups confectioners' sugar to the egg mixture and whisk until blended. Whisk in the chocolate mixture. Add the flour and whisk until smooth.

Spoon the batter evenly into the prepared soufflé dishes and bake for 14 to 16 minutes; the centers should be runny. Dust with confectioners' sugar to taste and serve warm with ice cream if desired.

As an alumna of Akron University, Sheila was a product development specialist for Bob Evans Farm Food Service until drawn to education. In eleven years at Tri-Rivers, Sheila has inspired students to become involved with FCCLA, Team Cuisine, and ProStart®. In 2003, she was named winner of the NRAEF ProStart® Teacher Excellence because of her commitment to the ProStart® programs.

Sheila Hamm
ProStart® Instructor
Tri-Rivers Career Center
Marion, Ohio

Flourless Cakes
Makes 150 (1½-inch) squares

- 5 pounds bittersweet chocolate, coarsely chopped
- 5 pounds butter, softened
- 5 pounds egg yolks
- 5 pounds egg whites
- 5 pounds sugar

Preheat the oven to 325 degrees for 20 to 25 minutes. Line the bottom of 6 sheet cake pans with baking parchment. Heat the chocolate in a double boiler until melted, stirring occasionally; keep warm. Beat the butter with a mixer fitted with a paddle attachment in a large mixing bowl until creamy. Add the egg yolks gradually, beating constantly until blended.

Beat the egg whites with a mixer fitted with a wire whip in a mixing bowl until foamy. Add the sugar gradually, beating constantly until stiff peaks form.

Add the warm chocolate to the yolk mixture and beat until blended, scraping the bowl occasionally. Fold in the egg whites and pour the batter evenly into the prepared pans, about 3 to 4 quarts per pan. Bake for 20 to 25 minutes or until the cakes test done.

Sara Thomas
Pastry Chef
Made From Scratch Catering
Plain City, Ohio

Deep Dark Chocolate Cake
Serves 12

CAKE
2 cups sugar
1 3/4 cups flour
3/4 cup baking cocoa
1 1/2 teaspoons baking powder
1 1/2 teaspoons baking soda
1 teaspoon salt
1 cup milk
1/2 cup vegetable oil
2 eggs
2 teaspoons vanilla extract
1 cup boiling water

ONE-BOWL CHOCOLATE BUTTERCREAM FROSTING
6 tablespoons butter
2 2/3 cups confectioners' sugar
1/2 cup baking cocoa
1/3 cup milk
1 teaspoon vanilla extract

For the cake, preheat the oven to 350 degrees. Spray two 9-inch cake pans or one 9×13-inch cake pan with nonstick cooking spray and coat with flour, shaking off the excess. Combine the sugar, 1 3/4 cups flour, the baking cocoa, baking powder, baking soda and salt in a mixing bowl and mix well. Add the milk, oil, eggs and vanilla and beat at medium speed for 2 minutes, scraping the bowl occasionally. Stir in the boiling water; the batter will be thin.

Pour the batter into the prepared pans. Bake for 30 to 35 minutes or until a wooden pick inserted in the center comes out clean. Cool in the pans on a wire rack.

For the frosting, beat the butter in a mixing bowl until light and fluffy. Add the confectioners' sugar, baking cocoa, milk and vanilla and beat until creamy and of a spreading consistency. Spread about 3/4 of the frosting between the layers and over the top and side of the cake. Let stand until dry. Spread the top and side of the cake with the remaining frosting.

Linda feels the ProStart® program is a wonderful opportunity for students to receive actual industry experience and training. Students are given many opportunities to network with professionals and work toward securing the National Certificate of Achievement and perhaps a scholarship for a post-secondary degree. In addition to being a Tri-Rivers Alumni of the Year, Linda earned the NRAEF 2002 Teacher Development Award from Buffets Inc.

Linda Golden
*ProStart® Instructor
Tri-Rivers Career Center*

Chocolate Espresso Cake
Serves 12

12 ounces semisweet chocolate, coarsely chopped
4 ounces unsweetened chocolate, coarsely chopped
2 cups (4 sticks) unsalted butter, sliced
1 cup espresso
1 cup packed brown sugar
8 eggs, lightly beaten
Confectioners' sugar to taste

Preheat the oven to 350 degrees. Line the bottom of a 9-inch cake pan with baking parchment. Place the chocolate in a large heatproof bowl. Combine the butter, espresso and brown sugar in a medium saucepan and bring to a boil, stirring occasionally. Boil until the brown sugar dissolves, stirring frequently. Pour the brown sugar mixture over the chocolate and whisk until smooth. Cool slightly and whisk in the eggs.

Pour the batter into the prepared pan and place the cake pan in a roasting pan. Add enough hot water to the roasting pan to come halfway up the side of the cake pan.

Bake for 1 hour or until the center is set and a wooden pick inserted in the center comes out with just a few moist crumbs attached. Remove the cake pan from the water and chill, covered, for 8 to 10 hours.

To serve, loosen the cake by running a sharp knife around the edge of the pan or warming the pan for approximately 15 seconds and invert onto a cake plate. Dust with confectioners' sugar. You may substitute 1 tablespoon instant espresso powder dissolved in 1 cup hot water for the espresso.

Russell Young
Executive Sous Chef
Hyatt on Capital Square
Columbus, Ohio

German Chocolate Cake
Serves 12

CAKE
2 cups flour
1 teaspoon baking soda
1/4 teaspoon salt
4 ounces German's sweet chocolate, coarsely chopped
1/2 cup water
2 cups sugar
1 cup (2 sticks) butter, softened
4 egg yolks
1 teaspoon vanilla extract
1 cup buttermilk
4 egg whites

CHOCOLATE BUTTERCREAM ICING AND ASSEMBLY
2 pounds confectioners' sugar
1 cup baking cocoa
6 tablespoons milk
2 teaspoons vanilla extract
1 cup (2 sticks) butter, softened
Cream Filling (page 19)
Coconut Pecan Filling (page 19)

For the cake, preheat the oven to 350 degrees. Grease and flour two 10-inch cake pans and line the bottoms with baking parchment. Mix 2 cups flour, the baking soda and salt together. Heat the chocolate and water in a double boiler until blended, stirring occasionally. Beat the sugar and butter in a mixing bowl until creamy, scraping the bowl occasionally. Add the egg yolks 1 at a time, beating until fluffy after each addition. Stir in the chocolate and vanilla. Beat in the flour mixture alternately with the buttermilk.

Beat the egg whites in a mixing bowl until stiff peaks form and fold into the chocolate batter.

Pour the batter evenly into the prepared cake pans and bake for 20 to 25 minutes or until the layers test done. Cool in the pans for 10 minutes. Remove to a wire rack to cool completely.

For the icing, mix the confectioners' sugar and baking cocoa in a bowl. Blend the milk and vanilla in a small bowl. Beat the butter in a mixing bowl until creamy, scraping the bowl occasionally. Add the baking cocoa mixture and milk mixture to the creamed butter alternately, mixing well after each addition.

To assemble, cut each layer into halves horizontally. Stack the layers on a plate, spreading the tops of alternate layers with Cream Filling and Coconut Pecan Filling. Ice the sides with the Chocolate Buttercream Icing.

Jennifer is a ProStart® student at Springfield Clark JVS. In addition to being chapter treasurer for FCCLA, she took second place in pastry arts at the regional competition. Jennifer is also active with Team Cuisine and received the 2004 Front of the House Award and was a member of the second-place team. Jennifer plans to attend Johnson and Wales University and ultimately open her own coffee shop/bakery.

Jennifer Schiller
Springfield Clark JVS '05
Springfield, Ohio

Cream Filling
Makes 1 1/2 cups

5 tablespoons flour
1 cup milk
1 cup sugar
1/2 cup (1 stick) butter, softened
1/2 cup shortening
1 teaspoon vanilla extract
1/2 teaspoon salt

Whisk the flour into the milk in a saucepan until blended. Bring to a boil and boil for 2 minutes or until thickened, stirring constantly. Let stand until cool. Beat the sugar, butter, shortening, vanilla and salt in a mixing bowl until creamy, scraping the bowl occasionally. Add the warm milk mixture to the creamed mixture and beat for 5 minutes or until the sugar dissolves, scraping the bowl occasionally.

Coconut Pecan Filling
Makes 2 cups

1 (14-ounce) can sweetened condensed milk
1/2 cup (1 stick) margarine
3 egg yolks, lightly beaten
1 1/3 cups shredded coconut
1 cup chopped pecans
1 teaspoon vanilla extract

Combine the condensed milk, margarine and egg yolks in a saucepan. Cook over medium heat for 10 minutes or until thickened, stirring constantly. Remove from the heat and stir in the coconut, pecans and vanilla. Let stand for 10 minutes before spreading.

Red Velvet Cake
Serves 12

2 1/4 cups cake flour
1 1/2 cups sugar
1/2 cup shortening
2 eggs
2 tablespoons baking cocoa
1/4 cup red food coloring
2 tablespoons water

1 cup buttermilk
1 teaspoon vanilla extract
1/4 teaspoon salt
1 tablespoon white vinegar
1 teaspoon baking soda
Red Velvet Icing (page 21)

Preheat the oven to 350 degrees. Sift the flour 2 or 3 times. Beat the sugar and shortening in a mixing bowl until light and fluffy, scraping the bowl occasionally. Add the eggs and beat for 1 minute.

Combine the baking cocoa, food coloring and water in a bowl and stir until a paste forms. Add the paste gradually to the egg mixture, beating constantly until blended. Gradually beat in a mixture of the buttermilk and vanilla.

Add the flour and salt and beat for 2 to 3 minutes, scraping the bowl occasionally. Mix the vinegar and baking soda in a small bowl and beat into the batter.

Spoon the batter into two 9-inch cake pans. Bake for 25 to 30 minutes or until the layers test done. Cool in the pans for 10 minutes. Remove to a wire rack to cool completely. Spread the Red Velvet Icing between the layers and over the top and side of the cake.

Debbie Blevins
Owner/Operator
Union Mills Confectionary
West Portsmouth, Ohio

Red Velvet Icing
Serves 12

1 cup sugar
5 tablespoons flour
1 cup milk
1 cup shortening or butter
1 cup confectioners' sugar
2 teaspoons vanilla extract

Combine the sugar and flour in a saucepan and mix well. Whisk in the milk until blended. Cook over medium heat until a thick paste forms, stirring constantly. Let stand until cool. Combine the paste mixture, shortening, confectioners' sugar and vanilla in a mixing bowl and beat for 5 minutes or until light and fluffy, scraping the bowl occasionally.

Texas Sheet Cake

Makes 2 dozen (2-inch) squares

CAKE
- 2 cups flour
- 2 cups sugar
- 1 cup water
- 1/2 cup shortening
- 1/2 cup (1 stick) margarine
- 5 tablespoons baking cocoa
- 2 eggs, beaten
- 1 tablespoon vanilla extract
- 1 tablespoon baking soda
- 1/2 cup sour cream

CHOCOLATE NUT FROSTING
- 1/2 cup (1 stick) margarine
- 1/2 cup milk
- 5 tablespoons baking cocoa
- 1 1/2 pounds (about) confectioners' sugar
- 1 cup chopped pecans

For the cake, preheat the oven to 350 degrees. Mix the flour and sugar in a heatproof bowl. Combine the water, shortening, margarine and baking cocoa in a saucepan and cook over low heat until blended, stirring frequently. Add the hot baking cocoa mixture to the flour mixture and mix well.

Whisk the eggs, vanilla and baking soda in a bowl until blended and stir into the flour mixture. Mix in the sour cream.

Spoon the batter into a 12×16-inch or 12×14-inch cake pan. Bake for 15 to 20 minutes or until the cake tests done. Cool in the pan on a wire rack.

For the frosting, bring the margarine, milk and baking cocoa to a boil in a saucepan, stirring frequently. Remove from the heat and add enough confectioners' sugar until of a spreading consistency and mix well. Stir in the pecans. Spread the frosting over the top of the cake.

Lillian Morrison
Abner's Country Restaurant
Reynoldsburg, Ohio

Warm Chocolate Cake
Serves 4

1/2 cup (1 stick) unsalted butter
4 ounces bittersweet chocolate, such as Valrhona
2 eggs
2 egg yolks
1/4 cup sugar
2 teaspoons flour

Preheat the oven to 450 degrees. Lightly butter four 4-ounce baking molds, custard cups or ramekins. Dust lightly with flour and tap off the excess and then repeat the process.

Heat 1/2 cup butter and the chocolate in a double boiler over simmering water for 15 minutes or until the chocolate is almost completely melted. Remove from the heat and whisk until combined.

Beat the eggs, egg yolks and sugar in a mixing bowl for 5 minutes or until thickened and pale yellow.

Add the egg mixture and 2 teaspoons flour to the chocolate mixture and whisk just until combined; do not overmix.

Spoon the batter evenly into the prepared molds and arrange the molds on a baking sheet. Bake for 7 to 10 minutes or until the sides are set but the center is still quite soft and jiggles when lightly touched. Remove from the oven and invert each mold onto a dessert plate. Let stand for about 30 seconds and unmold the cakes by lifting up 1 edge of the mold. The cakes will slide out onto the plates. Serve immediately.

Michelle Willoughby
Chef
The Ocean Club
Columbus, Ohio

Chocolate Cream Cheese Cake

Serves 8

1 (16-ounce) package chocolate brownie mix
16 ounces cream cheese, softened
1/3 cup sugar
2 tablespoons vanilla extract
8 ounces frozen whipped topping, thawed

Prepare and bake the brownies using the package directions for a 9×13-inch baking pan. Cool in the pan on a wire rack.

Beat the cream cheese, sugar and vanilla in a mixing bowl at medium speed until blended, scraping the bowl occasionally. Fold in 2 cups of the whipped topping and spread over the baked layer. Chill, covered, for 3 hours or until set.

Spread the remaining whipped topping over the prepared layers. Chill, covered, until serving time.

This recipe was developed by the student and her grandmother. This cake is on the menu in the student restaurant at North High School everyday and is the most popular dessert menu item.

Asten is a ProStart® student at North High School. Having earned the Career Excellence Award from Akron Public Schools as a junior, Asten wants to learn all she can so she can make the very best choices when she graduates. Her goal after going to culinary arts school is to become a master chef and open her own restaurant.

Asten Singletary
North High School '05
Akron, Ohio

Chocolate Malt Brownies
Serves 8 to 10

BROWNIES
1/2 cup flour
1/4 cup malted milk powder
1/2 cup (1 stick) unsalted butter, cubed
1 1/2 ounces semisweet chocolate, coarsely chopped
1 tablespoon vanilla extract
3 eggs
1/2 cup sugar
6 tablespoons heavy cream

CHOCOLATE SAUCE
1/2 cup heavy cream
1/4 cup milk
1/2 cup sugar
1/4 cup malted milk powder
1 1/2 ounces chocolate, coarsely chopped
2 tablespoons unsalted butter

For the brownies, preheat the oven to 350 degrees. Lightly butter 8 to 10 ramekins or soufflé baking cups. Sift the flour and malted milk powder together. Combine 1/2 cup butter and the chocolate in a double boiler and cook over low heat until melted, stirring constantly; whisk until smooth. Remove from the heat and stir in the vanilla.

Beat the eggs and sugar in a mixing bowl until pale yellow. Add the chocolate mixture gradually, stirring constantly until blended. Stir in the flour mixture and blend in the heavy cream.

Fill the prepared ramekins about 2/3 full and bake for 25 to 30 minutes or until a wooden pick inserted in the center comes out clean.

For the sauce, combine the heavy cream and milk in a saucepan and bring just to a boil, stirring occasionally. Add the sugar and malted milk powder and cook until the sugar dissolves, stirring frequently. Stir in the chocolate. Whisk in the butter and return to a boil; reduce the heat. Simmer for 10 to 15 minutes or until the desired consistency, stirring occasionally. Serve with the brownies.

Jonathan Adolph
Executive Chef
Strada World Cuisine
Columbus, Ohio

Berry Delicious Cake

Serves 12

14 ounces cake flour
14 ounces sugar
4 teaspoons baking powder
4 teaspoons salt
1 1/2 cups vegetable oil
2/3 cup egg yolks (8 yolks)
2/3 cup water

1 tablespoon vanilla extract
1 cup egg whites (8 whites)
White Chocolate Buttercream Icing (page 27)
Fresh raspberries, blueberries and strawberries
6 ounces white chocolate

Preheat the oven to 350 degrees. Grease and flour the bottoms of two 10-inch cake pans. Sift the flour, 1/3 of the sugar, the baking powder and salt into a bowl and mix well. Beat the oil and egg yolks in a mixing bowl just until combined. Stir in the water and vanilla. Add the flour mixture and beat at high speed for 1 minute.

Beat the egg whites in a mixing bowl until foamy. Add the remaining sugar gradually, beating constantly until stiff peaks form. Fold the meringue into the batter. Spoon the batter evenly into the prepared pans. Bake for 25 minutes or until the layers spring back when pressed lightly in the center. Invert the pans onto a wire rack and let stand in the pans until cool.

Cut each layer horizontally into halves. Spread each half with some of the icing. Stack the layers on a cake plate, spreading the raspberries, blueberries and strawberries in the order listed between the layers. Spread some of the icing over the top and side of the cake. Spoon the remaining icing into a pastry tube.

Score the cake lightly into 12 equal portions. Pipe an icing rosette in each portion, placing each on the edge of the cake, near the right scoring. Alternate a raspberry and a blueberry in each rosette. Place sliced strawberries in the center and garnish with white chocolate curls.

Artevia was a ProStart® student at Madison Comprehensive High School. In addition to earning three stars at the Family Career and Community Leaders of America regional competition for Pastry Arts, she then went on to earn two stars at the state competition. She is a recipient of the Banks-Willeke Scholarship from the Mid-Central Restaurant Association. Artevia plans on attending Sinclair Community College to study Culinary Arts. She wants to work in a restaurant where she can make creations come to life for her customers as she gives them her best.

Artevia Ware
Madison Comprehensive High School '04
Mansfield, Ohio

White Chocolate Buttercream Icing
Serves 12

18 ounces white chocolate, coarsely chopped
24 ounces cream cheese, softened
1 1/2 cups (3 sticks) unsalted butter, softened

Place the chocolate in a double boiler over hot water and cover with plastic wrap. Heat until the chocolate melts, stirring occasionally. Remove from the heat and stir until smooth. Let stand until cool.

Beat the cream cheese in a mixing bowl until smooth and creamy. Add the chocolate gradually, beating constantly until smooth. Add the butter and beat until blended and of a spreading consistency.

Carrot Cakes

Makes 3 cakes

1 cup raisins
4 1/2 cups pastry flour
4 teaspoons baking soda
4 teaspoons cinnamon
2 teaspoons salt
3 1/4 cups sugar
2 1/2 cups vegetable oil
8 eggs
6 cups finely shredded carrots
1 cup drained crushed pineapple
White Chocolate Frosting (page 29)

Combine the raisins with enough hot water to generously cover in a bowl. Let stand for 15 minutes and drain. Preheat the oven to 350 degrees. Line three 10-inch springform pans with baking parchment and coat the paper and sides of the pans with nonstick cooking spray. Sift the flour, baking soda, cinnamon and salt into a bowl and mix well.

Beat the sugar and oil in a mixing bowl until blended. Beat in the eggs 4 at a time. Fold in the flour mixture and then fold in the raisins, carrots and pineapple. Spoon the batter evenly into the prepared pans. Bake for 25 to 55 minutes or until a wooden pick inserted in the center comes out clean. Let stand until cool.

Cut each cake horizontally into 3 rounds. Spread the frosting over the top of each round and stack to make three 3-layer cakes. Chill, covered, until serving time.

Brian Wilson
Executive Chef
Cap City Fine Diner
Gahanna, Ohio

White Chocolate Frosting
Frosts 3 cakes

1 pound white chocolate, chopped
1 cup (2 sticks) unsalted butter
12 cups confectioners' sugar
12 ounces cream cheese, softened
1 1/2 cups (3 sticks) butter, softened
3 tablespoons vanilla extract
1/3 teaspoon salt

Combine the chocolate and 1 cup butter in a double boiler. Cook over simmering water until melted, stirring frequently. Remove from the heat. Beat the confectioners' sugar, cream cheese, 1 1/2 cups butter, the vanilla and salt in a mixing bowl until blended, scraping the bowl occasionally. Add the chocolate mixture and beat until smooth and of a spreading consistency.

Cinnamon-Grilled Pound Cake
Serves 10

2 cups cake flour
1/2 teaspoon nutmeg
1/2 teaspoon allspice
1/2 teaspoon salt
1 cup (2 sticks) butter, softened
1 cup sugar
4 egg yolks, at room temperature
1 teaspoon lemon juice

1 teaspoon vanilla extract
4 egg whites, at room temperature
2 cups mixed berries
1/2 cup sugar
1/2 cup cinnamon
1 cup sugar
1/2 cup (1 stick) butter, softened
1 cup whipping cream, whipped

Preheat the oven to 350 degrees. Mix the flour, nutmeg, allspice and salt together. Beat 1 cup butter and 1 cup sugar in a mixing bowl until creamy. Add the egg yolks, lemon juice and vanilla and beat until incorporated, scraping the bowl occasionally. Fold in the flour mixture.

Beat the egg whites in a mixing bowl until soft peaks form and fold into the batter. Spoon the batter into a greased and floured 5×9-inch loaf pan. Bake for 45 to 50 minutes or until the cake tests done.

Cool in the pan for 10 minutes and remove to a wire rack to cool completely. Cut the cake into 10 equal slices.

Combine the berries and 1/2 cup sugar in a bowl and mix gently. Mix the cinnamon and 1 cup sugar in a bowl. Spread both sides of each cake slice with 1/2 cup butter and coat with the sugar and cinnamon mixture. Arrange the slices on a baking sheet and grill or broil until caramelized. Top each serving with the berries and whipped cream.

Ken Schad
Henke Wine
Cincinnati, Ohio

Lemon Sponge with Raspberry Cream Filling
Serves 9

LEMON SPONGE
3/4 cup (heaping) superfine sugar
8 egg yolks
1 teaspoon grated lemon zest
1 teaspoon vanilla extract
1/16 teaspoon salt
8 egg whites
1/4 cup superfine sugar
1 1/4 cups flour, sifted
1/2 teaspoon vanilla extract
5 tablespoons butter, melted

RASPBERRY CREAM FILLING AND ASSEMBLY
3 cups whipping cream
1/4 cup sugar
1 cup simple syrup
1/2 cup raspberry preserves
1 1/2 pints fresh raspberries

For the sponge, preheat the oven to 350 degrees. Generously butter and flour three 8-inch cake pans. Combine 3/4 cup superfine sugar, the egg yolks, lemon zest, 1 teaspoon vanilla and salt in a heatproof mixing bowl and place over a pan of hot water. Whisk until the mixture is tepid. Beat with a mixer until light and fluffy.

Beat the egg whites and 1/4 cup superfine sugar in a mixing bowl until fluffy. Fold in the flour and egg whites in alternate batches. Fold in 1/2 teaspoon vanilla and the butter. Spoon the batter into the prepared pans. Bake for 25 to 30 minutes or until a wooden pick inserted in the center comes out clean. Cool in the pans for 10 minutes. Remove to a wire rack to cool completely.

For the filling, beat the whipping cream in a chilled mixing bowl at medium speed until soft peaks form. Add the sugar and beat until medium peaks form.

To assemble, brush each cake layer with simple syrup and spread 2 layers with the raspberry preserves. Spread a thin layer of whipped cream over the preserves. Layer with some of the raspberries and another thin layer of whipped cream.

Stack the filled layers and top with the third layer. Frost the top and side with the remaining whipped cream and garnish with the remaining raspberries.

Carl Quagliata
Ristorante Giovanni's
Mayfield Village, Ohio

Mandarin Orange Cake
Serves 12

CAKE
1 (2-layer) package butter cake mix
1/2 cup vegetable oil
4 eggs
1 (11-ounce) can mandarin oranges

PINEAPPLE FROSTING
1 (22-ounce) can crushed pineapple, chilled
2 (4-ounce) packages vanilla instant pudding mix
8 ounces whipped topping

For the cake, preheat the oven to 350 degrees. Grease and flour three 8-inch cake pans or one 9×13-inch cake pan. Combine the cake mix, oil and eggs in a mixing bowl and beat until blended. Add the undrained mandarin oranges and mix gently by hand so the oranges will retain their shape or beat in the oranges with a mixer just for flavor and not for texture.

Spoon the batter into the prepared pans and bake for 25 to 30 minutes or until a wooden pick inserted in the center comes out clean. Cool in the pans for 10 minutes. Remove to a wire rack to cool completely.

For the frosting, combine the undrained pineapple and pudding mix in a bowl and mix well. Fold in the whipped topping. Spread the frosting between the layers and over the top and side of the cake. Chill, covered, until serving time.

Karen Engum
N.E. Regional Internship Coordinator
Ohio Hospitality Educational Foundation
Akron, Ohio

Pumpkin Roll
Serves 6 to 8

CAKE
1 cup sugar
3/4 cup flour
1 teaspoon cinnamon
1 teaspoon salt
1 teaspoon baking soda
2/3 cup pumpkin
3 eggs
Confectioners' sugar to taste

CREAM CHEESE FILLING AND ASSEMBLY
8 ounces cream cheese, softened
1 cup confectioners' sugar
1 tablespoon margarine
1 teaspoon vanilla extract

For the cake, preheat the oven to 350 degrees. Grease a 10×15-inch baking pan and line with waxed paper. Combine the sugar, flour, cinnamon, salt and baking soda in a bowl and mix well. Add the pumpkin and eggs and mix until blended.

Spread the batter in the prepared pan and bake for 9 to 12 minutes or until the cake tests done. Invert the cake onto a tea towel dusted heavily with confectioners' sugar and discard the waxed paper.

Roll the warm cake in the towel as for a jelly roll from the short side and place on a wire rack to cool.

For the filling, beat the cream cheese, confectioners' sugar, margarine and vanilla in a mixing bowl until creamy, scraping the bowl occasionally.

To serve, unroll the cooled cake carefully and remove the towel. Spread the filling to within 1 inch of the edge and reroll. Wrap in plastic wrap or foil and chill until serving time.

Amy Magi
Baker
Phil's Inn Restaurant
Port Clinton, Ohio

Piña Colada Party Cakes
Serves 6

1 (8-ounce) can crushed pineapple
1 2/3 cups flour
1/3 cup sugar
2 1/4 teaspoons baking powder
1/4 teaspoon salt
3/4 cup cream of coconut
1/4 cup vegetable oil
1 egg
Pineapple Frosting (page 35)
Shredded coconut (optional)

Preheat the oven to 325 degrees. Spray 6 muffin cups with nonstick cooking spray and line with cupcake liners. Drain the pineapple, reserving 1/4 cup of the juice for the Pineapple Frosting.

Combine the flour, sugar, baking powder and salt in a bowl and mix well. Make a well in the center of the flour mixture.

Whisk the cream of coconut, oil and egg in a bowl until blended. Add the cream of coconut mixture to the well and stir just until moistened. Fold in the pineapple. Fill the prepared muffin cups 1/3 full. Bake for 15 minutes and remove immediately to a wire rack to cool. Spread the cakes with the Pineapple Frosting and sprinkle with coconut.

Michelle was a ProStart® student at Tri-Rivers and received a gold medal in the 2004 regional FCCLA dining room attendant competition. Michelle's plans include furthering her education in pastry and baking with a goal of one day owning her own bread and pastry shop.

Michelle Spradlin
Tri-Rivers Career Center '04
Marion, Ohio

Pineapple Frosting
Makes 1 cup

2/3 cup sugar
1/4 cup pineapple juice (reserved from Piña Colada Party Cakes)
1 egg white, lightly beaten
1 tablespoon light corn syrup
1/16 teaspoon cream of tartar
1/16 teaspoon salt
1/2 teaspoon pineapple extract
1/2 teaspoon strawberry extract

Combine the sugar, pineapple juice, egg white, corn syrup, cream of tartar and salt in a small saucepan and mix well. Cook over medium-low heat until blended, stirring frequently. Beat with a mixer for 7 minutes or until medium peaks form. Remove from the heat and beat in the flavorings.

Torte
Serves 12

CHOCOLATE PUDDING ICING
1 (6-ounce) package chocolate pudding and pie filling mix
3 tablespoons (heaping) cornstarch
1 tablespoon baking cocoa
Milk
1/2 recipe Buttercream Icing (page 37)

VANILLA PUDDING ICING
1 (6-ounce) package vanilla pudding and pie filling mix
3 tablespoons (heaping) cornstarch
Milk
1/2 recipe Buttercream Icing (page 37)

CAKE AND ASSEMBLY
1 (2-layer) package yellow butter cake mix
Raspberry Filling (page 37)

For the chocolate icing, combine the pudding mix, cornstarch and baking cocoa in a saucepan and mix well. Add milk according to the package directions and cook using the package directions. Cool slightly and chill, covered, in the refrigerator. Beat in the icing and chill for 1 day.

For the vanilla icing, combine the pudding mix and cornstarch in a saucepan and mix well. Add milk according to the package directions and cook using the package directions. Cool slightly and chill, covered, in the refrigerator. Beat in the icing and chill for 1 day.

For the cake, prepare and bake the cake using the package directions for two 9-inch cake pans. Cool in the pans for 10 minutes and remove to a wire rack to cool completely. Cut each layer horizontally into halves.

To assemble, place 1 cake half on a cake plate and spread with a thin layer of Raspberry Filling and some of the vanilla pudding icing. Layer with another cake half and spread with a thin layer of Raspberry Filling and some of the chocolate pudding icing. Repeat this layering process with the remaining cake halves, Raspberry Filling, most of the vanilla icing and most of the chocolate icing. Spread the remaining chocolate icing over the top of the cake and pipe the remaining vanilla icing in a decorative pattern over the top of the cake.

Carli Brant
Trumbull County JVS
Warren, Ohio

Buttercream Icing
Serves 12

1 cup (2 sticks) unsalted butter
1 cup confectioners' sugar

Beat the butter in a mixing bowl until creamy, scraping the bowl occasionally. Add the confectioners' sugar and beat until stiff. Chill, covered, in the refrigerator until firm.

Raspberry Filling
Serves 12

2 cups raspberries
1/2 cup sugar
2 tablespoons water

Combine the raspberries, sugar and water in a heavy saucepan. Cook over medium heat for 20 minutes or until thickened to the desired consistency. Spoon into a bowl, cover and chill in the refrigerator.

Chocolate Cheesecake

Chocolate Mascarpone Cheesecake

Coconut Cheesecake with Macadamia Crust

Crème Brûlée Cheesecake

Guinness Cheesecake

Miniature Cheesecakes with Lemon Marmalade

Pecan Cheesecake

Praline-Crusted Cheesecake

Sour Cream Cheesecake

Sweet Potato Cheesecake

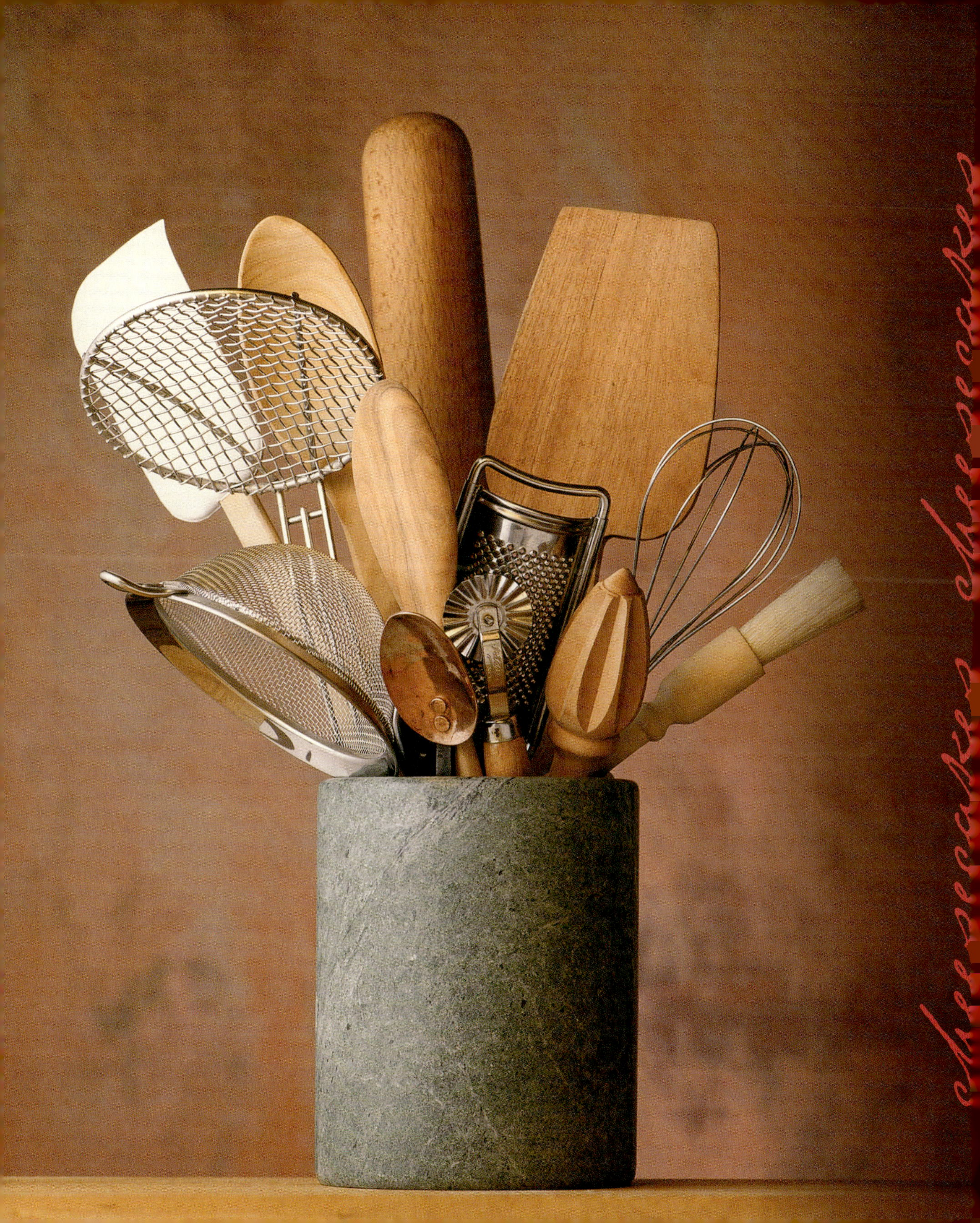
cheesecakes cheesecakes

Chocolate Cheesecake
Serves 12

10 ounces bittersweet or semisweet chocolate, coarsely chopped
1 cup (2 sticks) unsalted butter
1 1/4 cups sugar
5 eggs
5 tablespoons flour
1 1/2 teaspoons baking powder

Preheat the oven to 325 degrees. Heat the chocolate and butter in a heavy saucepan over low heat until blended, stirring frequently. Remove from the heat. Beat the sugar and eggs in a mixing bowl until blended and slightly thickened. Sift the flour and baking powder over the egg mixture and fold in. Gradually fold in the chocolate mixture.

Spoon the batter into a 10-inch springform pan sprayed with nonstick cooking spray. Bake for 20 minutes and cover with foil. Bake for 30 minutes longer or until a wooden pick inserted in the center comes out with moist crumbs. Remove the foil and cool on a wire rack; the cake will fall. Serve with whipped cream and berries.

Debbie Lackey
Happy Chicken/Merry Milk Maid
Columbus, Ohio

Chocolate Mascarpone Cheesecake
Serves 12

CHOCOLATE GRAHAM CRACKER CRUST
1 1/2 cups graham cracker crumbs
1/2 cup sugar
1/4 cup baking cocoa
1/2 cup (1 stick) butter, melted

CHOCOLATE FILLING
16 ounces cream cheese, softened
1 3/4 cups sugar
1 teaspoon vanilla extract
16 ounces mascarpone cheese
6 eggs
7 ounces bittersweet chocolate, melted

For the crust, combine the graham cracker crumbs, sugar and baking cocoa in a bowl and mix well. Add the butter and stir until crumbly. Press the crumb mixture over the bottom and up the side of a 9-inch springform pan.

For the filling, preheat the oven to 350 degrees. Beat the cream cheese, sugar and vanilla in a mixing bowl until light and fluffy, scraping the bowl occasionally. Add the mascarpone cheese and beat until blended. Add the eggs 1 at a time, mixing well after each addition.

Combine 1/2 of the cream cheese mixture with the chocolate in a bowl and mix well. Spread the chocolate mixture in the prepared pan and top with the remaining cream cheese mixture. Gently fold the 2 filling layers together with a spoon to create a marbleized effect. Bake in a water bath for 1 3/4 hours. Cool in the pan on a wire rack. Chill for 8 to 10 hours before serving.

Anthony Romano
Executive Chef
Players on Madison
Lakewood, Ohio

Coconut Cheesecake with Macadamia Crust
Serves 12

MACADAMIA CRUST
1 to 2 tablespoons unsalted butter, melted
1 cup graham cracker crumbs
1/4 cup macadamia nuts, toasted and coarsely chopped
1/4 cup (1/2 stick) unsalted butter, melted

FILLING
32 ounces cream cheese, softened
1 1/2 cups sugar
4 eggs
1/4 cup sour cream
1/2 cup unsweetened cream of coconut
2 tablespoons heavy cream
1 cup shredded sweetened coconut
Mango Sauce (optional)
Fresh strawberries, cut into halves (optional)

For the crust, brush the side of a 9-inch springform pan with 1 to 2 tablespoons butter. Combine the graham cracker crumbs, macadamia nuts and 1/4 cup butter in a bowl and mix well. Press the crumb mixture over the bottom of the prepared pan. Wrap the bottom of the pan with foil and chill for 15 minutes or until the crust is set.

For the filling, preheat a conventional oven to 350 degrees or a convection oven to 325 degrees. Beat the cream cheese in a mixing bowl until light and fluffy. Add the sugar and beat until smooth, scraping the bowl occasionally. Add the eggs 1 at a time, mixing well after each addition.

Beat in the sour cream, cream of coconut and heavy cream until blended. Spoon the cream cheese mixture into the prepared pan and sprinkle with the coconut.

Place the springform pan in a larger baking pan. Add enough hot water to the baking pan to come halfway up the side of the springform pan. Bake for 1 1/4 hours or until set. Cool in the pan on a wire rack. Chill for 8 to 10 hours before serving. Slice the cheesecake and drizzle each serving with Mango Sauce; garnish with strawberries. Store the leftovers in a refrigerator. Prepare Mango Sauce by puréeing fresh mangoes with sugar to taste.

Andrew Draganski
Chef
Stixx Asia Bistro
Sylvania, Ohio

Crème Brûlée Cheesecake
Serves 10

2 quarts heavy cream
15 ounces sugar
1 1/2 teaspoons vanilla bean scrapings
13 ounces pasteurized egg yolks, beaten
1 tablespoon poppy seeds, toasted
Butter, softened
1/2 ounce graham cracker crumbs
24 ounces cream cheese, softened

2 teaspoons vanilla bean scrapings
11 ounces sugar
9 1/2 ounces eggs
2 1/4 cups sour cream
5 tablespoons superfine sugar
5 tablespoons raw sugar
Crème Anglaise
10 fresh strawberries with hulls

Combine the heavy cream, 15 ounces sugar and 1 1/2 teaspoons vanilla bean scrapings in a saucepan and mix well. Cook until hot but not boiling, stirring occasionally. Stir 2 cups of the hot cream mixture into the egg yolks gradually; stir the egg yolk mixture into the hot cream mixture. Cook over medium heat until thickened, stirring frequently. Strain into a bowl, discarding the solids, and stir in the poppy seeds. Place the bowl in a larger bowl filled with ice and stir until chilled.

Sprinkle the graham cracker crumbs into a buttered 9-inch springform pan, shaking to remove the excess. Combine the cream cheese and 2 teaspoons vanilla bean scrapings in a mixing bowl and beat with a mixer fitted with a paddle attachment at medium speed for 2 minutes or until creamy. Add 11 ounces sugar and blend for 3 minutes. Add the eggs gradually, beating constantly. Beat at medium speed for 25 to 30 seconds.

Turn off the mixer and add the sour cream. Beat at low speed for 30 to 40 seconds or just until blended.

Preheat a convection oven to 300 degrees. Spread the cream cheese mixture in the prepared pan and place in a larger baking pan. Add enough hot water to reach halfway up the side of the springform pan. Bake for 1 hour and 15 minutes to 1 hour and 25 minutes or until the top begins to crack and a wooden pick inserted in the center comes out clean. Turn off the oven and let stand in the closed oven for 1 hour. Cool to room temperature on a wire rack. Chill, covered with plastic wrap, for 8 to 10 hours.

Mix the superfine sugar and raw sugar in a bowl. Slice the cheesecake into 10 slices and arrange on dessert plates. Spoon 3 tablespoons Crème Anglaise over each slice, allowing the excess to run onto the plate. Sprinkle each slice with 1 tablespoon of the sugar mixture. Caramelize with a culinary torch until golden brown. Garnish with the strawberries and serve.

Sean Schmidt
Chef
Parkers Blue Ash Grill
Blue Ash, Ohio

Guinness Cheesecake
Serves 12

VANILLA WAFER CRUST
1 1/2 cups fine vanilla wafer crumbs
3 tablespoons sugar
6 tablespoons unsalted butter, melted

BEER SYRUP
4 cups Guinness beer
1 3/4 cups sugar

CREAM CHEESE FILLING
32 ounces cream cheese, softened
3 tablespoons flour
2 teaspoons vanilla extract
4 eggs

For the crust, preheat the oven to 350 degrees. Combine the vanilla wafer crumbs, sugar and butter in a bowl and stir until crumbly. Pat the crumb mixture over the bottom of a 10-inch springform pan and bake for 5 to 7 minutes. Let stand until cool. Maintain the oven temperature.

For the syrup, bring the beer to a boil in a saucepan and boil until reduced to 1 cup. Stir in the sugar and cook just until the sugar dissolves, stirring frequently. Pour the syrup mixture into a small heatproof bowl and place the bowl over ice. Stir until completely cool.

For the filling, beat the cream cheese in a mixing bowl until smooth. Sift in the flour and beat until blended. Beat in the vanilla. Add the eggs 1 at a time, mixing well after each addition. Add the syrup gradually, beating constantly until smooth and creamy and scraping the bowl as needed.

Spread the filling over the baked layer and bake for 10 minutes. Reduce the oven temperature to 275 degrees and bake for 2 to 2 1/2 hours or until a wooden pick inserted in the center comes out clean. Cool in the pan on a wire rack for 1 hour. Chill for 8 to 10 hours before serving.

Jonathan Adolph
Executive Chef
Strada World Cuisine
Columbus, Ohio

Miniature Cheesecakes with Lemon Marmalade

Serves 2

VANILLA WAFER CRUST
1/2 cup fine vanilla wafer crumbs
2 tablespoons unsalted butter, melted

LEMON MARMALADE
2 lemons
1/2 cup sugar
1/4 cup lemon juice

CREAM CHEESE FILLING
8 ounces cream cheese, softened
1/4 cup sugar
1 tablespoon flour
2 eggs
2 tablespoons heavy cream
1/4 teaspoon vanilla extract

For the crust, preheat the oven to 350 degrees. Combine the vanilla wafer crumbs and butter in a bowl and mix well. Press the crumb mixture over the bottoms of two 4-inch springform pans. Bake for 8 minutes or until set. Let stand until cool. Reduce the oven temperature to 225 degrees.

For the marmalade, zest the lemons and cut the zest into short lengths. Remove the white pith from the lemons with a sharp knife. Separate into sections, discarding the membranes. Combine the lemon zest, lemon pulp, sugar and lemon juice in a saucepan and mix well. Simmer over low to medium heat for 1 1/4 hours or until slightly reduced, stirring occasionally. Remove from the heat and let stand until cool. Chill, covered, for 8 to 10 hours.

For the filling, combine the cream cheese, sugar and flour in a mixing bowl. Beat with a mixer fitted with a paddle attachment at medium speed until smooth, scraping the bowl occasionally. Add 1 of the eggs and beat at low speed until blended. Turn off the mixer and scrape the bowl. Add the remaining egg and beat at low speed until incorporated. Beat in the heavy cream and vanilla. Spoon the filling evenly into the prepared pans and bake for 1 hour. Run a sharp knife around the edge of the cheesecake and chill, uncovered, for 8 to 10 hours.

To serve, arrange the cheesecakes on individual dessert plates and drizzle with the marmalade. Also great served with fresh raspberries.

Jeffrey Robinson
Jack's Steakhouse at the Cleveland Airport
Marriott Hotel
Cleveland, Ohio

Pecan Cheesecake
Serves 12

PECAN CRUST
1/2 cup (1 stick) butter
1 cup flour
1 cup finely chopped pecans

CHOCOLATE FILLING
8 ounces cream cheese, softened
1 cup confectioners' sugar
1 cup whipped topping
1 (4-ounce) package chocolate instant pudding mix
3 (4-ounce) packages vanilla instant pudding mix
3 cups milk
2 cups whipped topping
2 tablespoons chopped pecans

For the crust, preheat the oven to 350 degrees. Cut the butter into the flour in a bowl until crumbly. Stir in the pecans. Press the crumb mixture over the bottom of a 9×13-inch baking pan. Bake for 15 minutes. Let stand until cool.

For the filling, beat the cream cheese, confectioners' sugar and 1 cup whipped topping in a mixing bowl until smooth.

Whisk the chocolate pudding mix, vanilla pudding mixes and milk in a bowl until blended. Add the cream cheese mixture to the pudding mixture and stir until smooth. Spoon the cream cheese mixture into the prepared pan and spread with 2 cups whipped topping. Sprinkle with the pecans and chill, covered, until serving time.

Mary is the ProStart® instructor for Kettering Fairmont High School Career Tech Center. She believes ProStart® is a fantastic opportunity for her students to learn about and become part of the food service industry. Her students are hands-on learners, and ProStart® gives them opportunities to learn and grow in a learning environment that stresses hands-on learning. In addition, the educational opportunities from scholarships to earning college credits makes this program a comprehensive approach to preparing students for the future.

Mary Minor Fowler
ProStart® Instructor
Kettering Fairmont High School
Career Tech Center
Kettering, Ohio

Praline-Crusted Cheesecake
Serves 12

PRALINE CRUST
2 cups shortbread cookie crumbs
3 tablespoons butter, melted
4 pralines, coarsely crumbled

CREAM CHEESE FILLING
8 ounces cream cheese, softened
1 3/4 cups sugar
2 tablespoons flour
1 1/2 teaspoons vanilla extract
4 eggs
2 extra-large egg yolks
1/3 cup whipped cream
1 teaspoon grated lemon zest

SOUR CREAM TOPPING AND GARNISH
2 cups sour cream
1/3 cup sugar
Crushed pralines

For the crust, preheat the oven to 350 degrees. Combine the cookie crumbs and butter in a bowl and mix well. Press the crumb mixture over the bottom and up the side of a greased 10-inch springform pan. Bake for 8 minutes. Let stand until cool and sprinkle with the pralines. Maintain the oven temperature.

For the filling, beat the cream cheese in a mixing bowl at medium speed until creamy. Add the sugar, flour and vanilla gradually and beat until smooth. Beat in the eggs and egg yolks. Stir in the whipped cream and lemon zest.

Spread the cream cheese mixture over the baked layer. Bake for 10 minutes. Reduce the oven temperature to 325 degrees and bake for 1 hour and 20 minutes longer. Cool for 1 hour.

For the topping, preheat the oven to 325 degrees. Mix the sour cream and sugar in a bowl and spread over the baked layer. Bake for 10 minutes. Let stand until cool and chill for 8 hours. Slice the cheesecake and sprinkle each serving with crushed pralines.

Sandy Sanders
Ricardo's
Columbus, Ohio

Sour Cream Cheesecake

Serves 20

GRAHAM CRACKER CRUST
1 1/2 cups graham cracker crumbs
1/2 cup sugar
1/2 cup (1 stick) butter, melted
1 teaspoon vanilla extract

CREAM CHEESE FILLING
24 ounces cream cheese, softened
1 cup sugar
5 eggs
1 teaspoon vanilla extract

SOUR CREAM TOPPING
2 cups sour cream
1/2 cup sugar
1 teaspoon vanilla extract

For the crust, grease a 9×13-inch baking dish. Combine the graham cracker crumbs, sugar, butter and vanilla in a bowl and mix well. Press the crumb mixture over the bottom of the prepared dish.

For the filling, preheat the oven to 300 degrees. Combine the cream cheese, sugar, eggs and vanilla in a mixing bowl and beat until blended but not completely smooth.

Spread the cream cheese mixture over the prepared layer and bake for 1 hour. Cool on a wire rack for 30 minutes.

For the topping, preheat the oven to 400 degrees. Mix the sour cream, sugar and vanilla in a bowl and spread over the baked layer. Bake for 10 to 12 minutes. Let stand until cool and chill until serving time.

Mindy Lacy
Rooster's Restaurant
Columbus, Ohio

Sweet Potato Cheesecake
Serves 12

VANILLA WAFER CRUST
2 cups vanilla wafer crumbs
   (8 ounces vanilla wafers)
1/3 cup butter or margarine, melted

CREAM CHEESE FILLING
24 ounces cream cheese, softened
3/4 cup sugar
1/2 cup packed brown sugar
3 eggs, lightly beaten
2 cups mashed cooked sweet potatoes
1/4 cup evaporated milk
1 1/2 teaspoons nutmeg
1 teaspoon each vanilla extract,
   cinnamon and fresh lemon juice

SOUR CREAM TOPPING
2 cups sour cream, at room temperature
1/4 cup sugar
2 teaspoons vanilla extract

For the crust, preheat the oven to 350 degrees. Toss the vanilla wafer crumbs with the butter in a bowl. Press over the bottom and 1 inch up the side of a buttered and floured 9 1/2- or 10-inch springform pan. Bake for 12 minutes. Let stand until cool. Reduce the oven temperature to 325 degrees.

For the filling, beat the cream cheese in a mixing bowl until smooth. Add the sugar and brown sugar and beat until blended. Add the eggs 1 at a time, mixing well after each addition and scraping the bowl occasionally.

Combine the sweet potatoes, evaporated milk, nutmeg, vanilla, cinnamon and lemon juice in a bowl and mix well. Add to the cream cheese mixture and beat until smooth.

Wrap foil loosely around the bottom and up the side of the springform pan. Spread the filling over the baked layer and place the springform pan in a larger baking dish or roasting pan. Arrange the baking dish on the middle oven rack. Add enough hot water to the baking dish to measure 1 inch. Bake for 70 minutes or until the edge is firm and the center trembles slightly. Remove the cheesecake from the water. Maintain the oven temperature.

For the topping, combine the sour cream, sugar and vanilla in a bowl and mix well. Spread over the baked layer and bake for 10 minutes longer. Cool on a wire rack for 1 hour. Remove the foil and the side of the pan and chill for 4 to 10 hours.

Anna Mae Tolson
Grandview Restaurant
Canfield, Ohio

Raspberry Crème Brûlée
Vanilla Crème Brûlée
Crème Brûlée
Baked Chocolate Mousse
Chocolate Mousse with Raspberry Coulis
Chocolate Mousse
Callebaut White Chocolate Godiva Mousse
Caramel Apple Bread Pudding
Bread Pudding
Bread Pudding with Cinnamon-Sugar Topping
Peach Croissant Bread Pudding
Honey Kahlúa Semifreddo
Date Pudding
Toffee Caramel Flan
Eggs in Snow
Panna Cotta
Buttermilk and Coconut Panna Cotta
Brandied Tiramisù
Tiramisù

custards
mousses
puddings

custodo mondeo puddingo

Raspberry Crème Brûlée
Serves 8

6 eggs
3/4 cup sugar
2 cups half-and-half
2 cups heavy cream
1 pint fresh raspberries
Sugar to taste

Preheat the oven to 450 degrees. Break the eggs into a bowl and add 3/4 cup sugar. Whisk for 1 minute or until smooth. Add the half-and-half and heavy cream and whisk until blended. Pour the egg mixture into eight 6-ounce ramekins and add about 5 raspberries to each ramekin.

Place the ramekins in a large baking pan and add enough hot water to the baking pan to measure 1 inch. Bake for 20 minutes.

Remove the ramekins from the water and let stand until cool. Sprinkle each custard with sugar to taste and caramelize with a culinary torch until golden brown. Serve immediately. You may prepare the custards in advance and store in the refrigerator, glazing just before serving.

Jack Edwards, CEC
Adams Mark Hotel
Columbus, Ohio

Vanilla Crème Brûlée
Serves 12

1 vanilla bean
4 cups heavy cream
1 cup egg yolks
1 cup packed brown sugar
2 tablespoons sugar
2 tablespoons brown sugar

Split the vanilla bean lengthwise into halves and scrape out the pulp with the tip of a knife. Combine the vanilla bean, vanilla pulp and 1 cup of the heavy cream in a saucepan and bring to a simmer. Remove from the heat and let steep for 10 minutes.

Preheat the oven to 325 degrees. Whisk the remaining 3 cups heavy cream, egg yolks and 1 cup brown sugar in a bowl until combined. Add the vanilla cream gradually, whisking constantly until blended. You may prepare to this point up to 5 days in advance and store, covered, in the refrigerator.

Strain the cream mixture through a sieve, discarding the solids. Pour the strained cream mixture into approximately twelve 4-ounce ramekins or baking cups. Arrange the ramekins in a large baking dish and add enough hot water to the baking dish to reach halfway up the sides of the ramekins. Cover the baking dish with foil and pierce the foil with a fork.

Bake for 30 minutes or until set. Remove to a wire rack to cool completely. Sprinkle the tops of the custards lightly with a mixture of the sugar and 2 tablespoons brown sugar. Caramelize with a culinary torch or broil until golden brown. Garnish with fresh fruit if desired.

Johnathan Beck
R.J. Snappers Bar & Grill
Columbus, Ohio

Crème Brûlée
Serves 8 to 10

4 cups heavy cream
1 cup sugar
12 egg yolks
1 vanilla bean, or 2 teaspoons vanilla extract

Preheat the oven to 275 degrees. Process the heavy cream, sugar, egg yolks and vanilla bean in a blender or with a hand blender until combined; skim off the foam. Pour the custard mixture into baking cups or ramekins.

Arrange the baking cups in a large baking pan and add enough hot water to the baking pan to reach halfway up the sides of the baking cups. Bake for 45 minutes or until set.

With a finance degree from Franklin University, a culinary degree from the Art Institute of Atlanta, and a master's degree from Ohio State University, Craig brings a wealth of knowledge to his position at Eastland Career Center and has enjoyed incorporating the ProStart® program into his curriculum. In addition to assistance from the Ohio Hospitality Educational Foundation, Craig is grateful for the support of the Central Ohio Restaurant Association with classroom speakers, internships, and competition coaches.

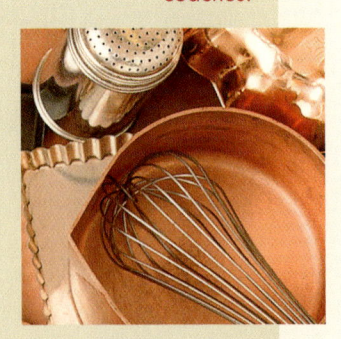

Craig Lomonico
ProStart® Instructor
Eastland Career Center
Groveport, Ohio

Baked Chocolate Mousse
Serves 12

1 1/2 pounds semisweet chocolate, coarsely chopped
1/2 cup (1 stick) plus 2 tablespoons unsalted butter
1 1/2 cups whipping cream
1/4 cup Frangelico
9 eggs

3/4 cup sugar
1/16 teaspoon salt
8 ounces hazelnut Granduja, or any high-quality milk chocolate
1 cup pirouette cookie crumbs
Whipped cream to taste

Preheat the oven to 325 degrees. Spray twelve 6-ounce muffin cups or soufflé cups with nonstick cooking spray and line with plastic wrap. Microwave the semisweet chocolate and butter in a microwave-safe dish until blended, stirring occasionally. Or you may heat in a double boiler. Cool slightly.

Beat the whipping cream and liqueur in a mixing bowl until stiff peaks form; do not overbeat. Beat the eggs and sugar in a mixing bowl for 5 minutes or until light and foamy. Fold 1/2 of the chocolate mixture into the egg mixture and fold the remaining chocolate mixture into the whipped cream mixture. Fold the egg mixture into the whipped cream mixture; do not overmix.

Fill the prepared muffin cups with the mousse mixture. Bake in a water bath for 30 to 35 minutes or until set but still moist in the centers when touched lightly. Cool for 5 minutes.

Place the hazelnut chocolate in a microwave-safe dish and microwave on Medium until melted, stirring every 20 seconds. Stir the cookie crumbs into the melted chocolate. Spread the chocolate crumb mixture on a foil-lined sheet pan and chill until set. Cut the chocolate into discs the size of the muffin cups using a round cutter.

Arrange 1 chocolate disc on each mousse and chill until completely cool. Invert the muffin cups onto a serving platter and garnish with whipped cream. Serve immediately.

Kim Hall
J. Pistone Market
Shaker Heights, Ohio

Chocolate Mousse with Raspberry Coulis

Serves 2

4 ounces bittersweet chocolate, coarsely chopped
1/4 cup (1/2 stick) butter
3 egg yolks
3 egg whites

5 ounces sugar
1/2 cup whipping cream
Raspberry Coulis (page 57)
Sugar Cages (page 57)

Combine the chocolate and butter in a double boiler and cook over low heat until blended, stirring occasionally. Cool slightly and whisk in the egg yolks 1 at a time until smooth.

Beat the egg whites in a mixing bowl until soft peaks form. Add the sugar gradually, beating constantly until stiff peaks form. Fold the egg whites into the chocolate mixture.

Beat the whipping cream in a mixing bowl until soft peaks form and fold into the chocolate mixture until streaks of the egg white or whipped cream no longer appear. Chill until set.

Squeeze the Raspberry Coulis onto 2 dessert plates. Invert the Sugar Cages and place in the coulis. Spoon the mousse into the cages.

If you are concerned about using raw eggs, use eggs pasteurized in their shells or an equivalent amount of pasteurized egg substitute.

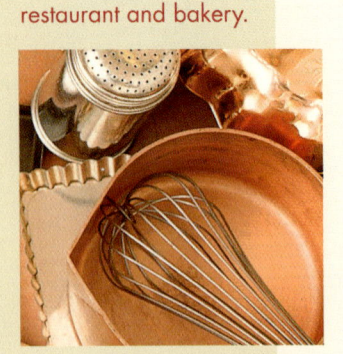

Matt was a ProStart® student at EHOVE Career Center and was a member of their culinary team for the 2004 Ohio Gordon Food Service ProStart® Student Competition. While serving his internship at the Invention Restaurant, Matt also found time to serve as president of FCCLA and become a junior member of the American Culinary Federation, EHOVE Leadership Program, and 5th Quarter Program. Matt will be attending Sullivan University majoring in culinary and pastry arts. Upon graduation, he would like to travel to major cities in the United States to hone his craft and to one day study under a master chef in France and Italy. His ultimate goal is to open his own restaurant and bakery.

Matt Sanders
EHOVE Career Center '04
Milan, Ohio

Raspberry Coulis
Serves 2

4 ounces fresh raspberries
2 tablespoons sugar
1 tablespoon lemon juice

Press the raspberries and sugar through a food mill to purée. Strain the raspberry mixture through a sieve into a saucepan, pressing on the solids to release all of the liquids; discard the solids. Stir in the lemon juice and cook over medium heat for 5 minutes or until reduced, stirring occasionally. Remove from the heat and pour into a squeeze bottle. Chill in the refrigerator.

Sugar Cages
Makes 2

2/3 cup sugar
2/3 cup corn syrup
1/3 cup water

Combine the sugar, corn syrup and water in a saucepan and mix well. Cook until the mixture registers 312 degrees on a candy thermometer and is a brown syrupy consistency. Using a spoon sprayed with nonstick cooking spray, drizzle the sugar mixture evenly in a crisscross pattern over 2 soup cups sprayed with nonstick cooking spray, creating a web-like cage. Let stand until firm. Remove the sugar cages from the cups gently.

Chocolate Mousse
Serves 12

22 1/2 ounces bittersweet chocolate, coarsely chopped
1/2 cup plus 1 tablespoon water
9 egg yolks
1 cup sugar
1 cup sour cream
9 egg whites
1/2 cup sugar

Heat the chocolate and water in a double boiler until the chocolate melts, stirring occasionally. Combine the egg yolks and 1 cup sugar in a mixing bowl and beat with a mixer fitted with a whip attachment until light and fluffy. Add the chocolate mixture to the egg mixture and beat until blended. Pour into a bowl and fold in the sour cream.

Beat the egg whites and 1/2 cup sugar in a mixing bowl until soft peaks form. Fold the egg whites into the chocolate mixture and mix well. Spoon the mousse into a 9×13-inch dish and chill until set.

If you are concerned about using raw eggs, use eggs pasteurized in their shells, which are sold at some specialty food stores, or use an equivalent amount of pasteurized egg substitute.

Justin Whites
Chef
Jay's Restaurant
Dayton, Ohio

Callebaut White Chocolate Godiva Mousse
Serves 6

7 1/2 ounces Callebaut white chocolate, coarsely chopped
1/2 cup heavy cream
3 tablespoons Godiva liqueur
3 1/2 ounces sugar

6 egg yolks
1/2 cup heavy cream
6 gelatin sheets
2 cups whipping cream
6 egg whites

Combine the white chocolate, 1/2 cup heavy cream and the liqueur in a double boiler and heat until blended, stirring occasionally. Whisk the sugar, egg yolks and 1/2 cup heavy cream in a bowl until the sabayon is a thick ribbon. Continue to whisk over an ice bath.

Bloom the gelatin sheets in cold water and add to the chocolate mixture. Fold into the sabayon. Beat the whipping cream in a mixing bowl until soft to medium peaks form and fold into the chocolate mixture.

Beat the egg whites in a mixing bowl until soft peaks form and fold into the chocolate mixture. Scoop the mousse into martini glasses and chill until serving time.

If you are concerned about using raw eggs, use eggs pasteurized in their shells, which are sold at some specialty food stores, or use an equivalent amount of pasteurized egg substitute.

Anthony Phenis
Executive Chef
Pier W
Lakewood, Ohio

Caramel Apple Bread Pudding
Serves 24

18 slices cinnamon swirl bread
8 Granny Smith apples, peeled and cut into matchsticks
Juice of 2 lemons
1/4 cup (1/2 stick) unsalted butter
3 cups heavy cream
2 cups milk
12 eggs
2 cups sugar
3 tablespoons vanilla extract
1 tablespoon cinnamon
2 teaspoons salt
1 teaspoon nutmeg
48 ounces caramel ice cream topping
Crème Anglaise or whipped cream
Caramel sauce

Cut the bread slices into 3/4-inch cubes and spread the cubes in a single layer on a sheet pan. Let stand at room temperature for 8 to 10 hours. Preheat the oven to 325 degrees. Combine the apples with enough cold water to cover in a bowl and stir in the lemon juice. Coat twenty-four 8-ounce ramekins with the butter and arrange the ramekins in a large roasting pan. Whisk the heavy cream, milk, eggs, sugar, vanilla, cinnamon, salt and nutmeg in a bowl until blended. Add the bread cubes and toss to coat. Drain the apples.

Spoon 1 ounce of the caramel topping into each prepared ramekin. Layer each with approximately 1/3 cup of the apples, 1/3 cup of the bread cube mixture, 1 ounce of the caramel topping, 1/3 cup of the apples and 1/3 cup of the bread cube mixture.

Place the roasting pan on the center oven rack and fill the roasting pan with enough hot water to reach to within 1/2 inch of the tops of the ramekins. Bake, covered with foil, for 20 minutes; remove the foil. Bake for 20 minutes longer. Remove the ramekins to a wire rack to cool.

Invert the bread puddings onto dessert plates and drizzle each with 3 tablespoons Crème Anglaise or top with a dollop of whipped cream. Drizzle with caramel sauce. You may prepare in advance, store in the refrigerator and reheat as needed.

As Gordon Food Service Consulting Chef, Gerry provides the company and its customers with a high-level view of the food service industry from the culinary standpoint and also supports the areas of menu and recipe development. Gordon Food Service is a major contributor to the Ohio Hospitality Educational Foundation and is a premier sponsor of the GFS Ohio ProStart® Student Competition.

Gerry Ludwig, CEC
Consulting Chef
Gordon Food Service
Grand Rapids, Michigan

Bread Pudding
Serves 20

3/4 cup bourbon
1/4 cup vanilla extract
1 large package raisins
2 quarts milk
2 quarts half-and-half
1 quart eggs

18 ounces sugar
1 teaspoon kosher salt
1/2 cup (1 stick) butter
4 pounds assorted bread, cut into cubes, about 2 gallons
8 ounces walnut pieces
1 cup (2 sticks) butter

Combine the bourbon and vanilla in a bowl and mix well. Mix the raisins into the bourbon mixture and let stand for 1 hour. Whisk the milk, half-and-half, eggs, sugar and salt in a bowl until the sugar dissolves.

Preheat the oven to 350 degrees. Coat a roasting pan with 1/2 cup butter. Combine the undrained raisins, milk mixture and bread cubes in the prepared roasting pan and mix well. Sprinkle with the walnuts and dot with 1 cup butter.

Bake, covered with the lid or foil, for 1 hour and 20 minutes or until set. Remove the lid and bake until brown on the top. Serve warm topped with a scoop of ice cream and drizzled with chocolate sauce and/or caramel sauce.

Rob Romph
Chef
Claire's Winery
Middleburg Heights, Ohio

Bread Pudding with Cinnamon-Sugar Topping
Serves 8

CINNAMON-SUGAR TOPPING
1/4 cup sugar
1 1/3 teaspoons cinnamon

BREAD PUDDING
1 cup sugar
7 eggs
3 1/2 cups milk
3 1/2 cups cream
1 tablespoon vanilla extract
1 teaspoon nutmeg
1/3 teaspoon salt
3/4 loaf sliced white bread, cut into 1 1/2-inch cubes

For the topping, mix the sugar and cinnamon in a bowl.

For the pudding, preheat the oven to 375 degrees. Whisk the sugar and eggs in a bowl until blended. Add the milk, cream, vanilla, nutmeg and salt and whisk until incorporated. Add the bread cubes and stir until moistened. Let stand for 5 minutes.

Pour the bread mixture into a greased 9×13-inch baking pan and sprinkle with the topping. Bake for 45 to 55 minutes or until the top is golden brown and the center trembles slightly when lightly shaken. The internal temperature should register 165 degrees. Cool slightly and serve with caramel sauce, butterscotch sauce and/or French vanilla ice cream. Store the leftovers in the refrigerator.

Wayne Leonard
Chef
The Golden Jersey Inn
Yellow Springs, Ohio

Peach Croissant Bread Pudding
Serves 12

BREAD PUDDING
1 tablespoon butter
2 cups heavy cream
1 cup sugar
1/4 cup peach brandy
5 eggs
1 tablespoon vanilla extract
6 large croissants
2 cups chopped fresh or thawed frozen peaches
3 tablespoons butter

PEACH BRANDY SAUCE
1 teaspoon cornstarch
2 tablespoons water
2 cups peach nectar
1 cup sugar
2 tablespoons butter
1/4 cup peach brandy

For the pudding, preheat the oven to 350 degrees. Coat an 8×11-inch baking dish with 1 tablespoon butter. Whisk the heavy cream, sugar, brandy, eggs and vanilla in a bowl until blended and pour into the prepared baking dish.

Slice the croissants horizontally into halves and arrange the bottom halves over the cream mixture. Sprinkle with the peaches and top with the croissant tops, pushing down with a spoon to ensure the croissants are covered with the cream mixture. Dot with 3 tablespoons butter and cover with foil.

Place the baking dish in a larger baking pan and add enough hot water to the baking pan to reach halfway up the sides of the baking dish. Bake for 35 to 40 minutes and remove the foil. Bake for 10 to 15 minutes longer or until brown.

For the sauce, dissolve the cornstarch in the water in a bowl. Combine the cornstarch mixture, nectar, sugar and butter in a saucepan and mix well. Bring to a boil and boil for 1 minute, stirring frequently. Remove from the heat and stir in the brandy. Serve with the bread pudding.

Denise Denman
Chef
Shaw's Restaurant & Inn
Lancaster, Ohio

Honey Kahlúa Semifreddo

Serves 8 to 10

As a seventeen-year teacher of Culinary Arts and Restaurant Management, Chuck has attended many conferences and seminars. At a conference, he learned about ProStart® and was so excited about the program that when he came home, he gathered information and went to his superior and said, "Let's get this program and get started. . . now."

His background includes working on board ship with the stewards, pastry chefs, and catering. He started cooking at the age of two, and years later, he is still cooking and enjoying every minute. In his spare time, he enjoys conducting and performing in the community band and community theater as well as traveling and gardening.

1 envelope unflavored gelatin
1/4 cup black coffee, chilled
16 ounces cream cheese, softened
3 tablespoons Kahlúa or coffee flavoring
2 tablespoons honey

2 egg whites, at room temperature
2 tablespoons sugar
1 cup whipping cream, chilled
1 tablespoon honey
1 tablespoon vanilla extract

Line a 4×9-inch loaf pan with baking parchment or heavy-duty foil strips, allowing a 3- to 4-inch overhang. The strips not only cover the product while freezing but make removal for serving easier.

Sprinkle the gelatin over the coffee in a microwave-safe cup. Let stand for 5 minutes. Microwave for 1 minute and stir. Let stand until cool. Combine the cream cheese, liqueur and 2 tablespoons honey in a mixing bowl. Beat with a mixer fitted with a paddle attachment until light and fluffy, scraping the bowl and beaters twice.

Place the egg whites in a clean dry mixing bowl. Beat with a mixer fitted with a whip attachment at medium speed until the whites break up. Increase the speed to high while gradually adding the sugar and beat until peaks form. Remove the meringue to a clean bowl.

Place the whipping cream in the meringue mixing bowl and beat with a mixer fitted with a whip attachment until stiff peaks form, gradually adding 1 tablespoon honey and the vanilla.

Add the coffee mixture to the cream cheese mixture and beat with a mixer fitted with a whip attachment until blended. Fold in the meringue and whipped cream mixture. Spoon into the prepared pan and cover.

Freeze for 6 to 10 hours. Remove from the freezer 2 hours prior to serving and place in the refrigerator. Invert onto a serving plate and cut into 3/4-inch slices. Serve with caramel sauce, chocolate sauce or coffee syrup.

Chuck Haas
ProStart® Instructor
Kenmore High School
Akron, Ohio

Date Pudding
Serves 40

PUDDING
6 cups pitted dates
3 tablespoons butter
2 tablespoons baking soda
4 cups boiling water
6 eggs, lightly beaten
2 cups sugar
1 tablespoon vanilla extract
7 cups chopped walnuts
7 cups flour

BROWN SUGAR SAUCE
AND ASSEMBLY
4 cups water
3 cups packed brown sugar
2 1/2 tablespoons butter
1/4 teaspoon salt
1/2 cup clear gel
1/2 cup water
2 teaspoons vanilla extract
1 teaspoon maple extract
Whipped cream

For the pudding, combine the dates, butter and baking soda in a large heatproof bowl. Add the boiling water and mix well. Let stand for 1 hour. Preheat the oven to 275 degrees.

Stir the eggs, sugar, vanilla, walnuts and flour into the date mixture. Spoon the batter into a parchment-lined sheet pan. Bake for 50 minutes. Let stand until cool and cut into squares. Freeze in resealable plastic freezer bags until needed.

For the sauce, bring 4 cups water, the brown sugar, butter and salt to a boil in a large saucepan. Mix the clear gel with 1/2 cup water in a bowl and stir into the brown sugar mixture. Return to a boil, stirring occasionally, and remove from the heat. Stir in the flavorings. Let stand for 15 minutes.

Cool rapidly in an ice bath, checking to ensure that the temperature drops to 40 degrees within 4 hours or less. Drizzle the sauce over the pudding on dessert plates and top with a dollop of whipped cream. Store the sauce in sterilized jars with tight-fitting lids in the refrigerator.

Ida Mast
Kitchen Manager
The Amish Door Restaurant
Wilmot, Ohio

Toffee Caramel Flan

Serves 10

2 1/2 cups sugar
1 cup water
3 cups milk
3 cups heavy cream
2 cinnamon sticks
1 vanilla bean, split horizontally

8 eggs
4 egg yolks
6 ounces brown sugar
1 tablespoon molasses
2 tablespoons amaretto

Lightly grease 10 ramekins. Combine the sugar and water in a small heavy saucepan and bring to a boil. Boil until the sugar is deep golden brown in color. Immediately pour 2 tablespoons of the syrup into each prepared ramekin and tilt to ensure even coverage over the bottoms. Arrange the ramekins in a 2-inch-deep hotel baking pan.

Bring the milk, heavy cream, cinnamon sticks and vanilla bean to a boil in a large saucepan. Remove from the heat and cover. Let steep for 30 minutes. Whisk the eggs, egg yolks, brown sugar, molasses and liqueur in a bowl until combined.

Remove the cover from the milk mixture, return to the heat and bring to a boil. Whisk about 1/3 of the hot milk mixture into the egg mixture. Whisk the egg mixture into the hot milk mixture.

Preheat the oven to 325 degrees. Strain the custard through a fine mesh sieve into a bowl, discarding the solids. Pour the custard evenly into the prepared ramekins. Add enough warm water to the hotel pan to reach halfway up the sides of the ramekins. Bake for 30 to 40 minutes or until the custards tremble slightly in the centers. Remove from the water bath to a wire rack and cool slightly. Chill in the refrigerator.

To serve, run a small sharp knife around the edge of each custard, invert onto a dessert plate and give the ramekins a firm sideways shake. Garnish each with fresh fruit and/or caramelized almonds.

Yolanda is a ProStart® student at Tri-Rivers Career Center and upon graduation plans to earn a degree at a culinary school. Her ultimate goal is to develop her culinary and business skills so she can open her own restaurant.

Yolanda Sanchez
Tri-Rivers Career Center '05
Marion, Ohio

Eggs in Snow
Serves 4

3 egg whites
1/4 cup sugar
2 cups milk
3 egg yolks
1/4 cup sugar
1/8 teaspoon salt
1 teaspoon vanilla extract, rum or dry sherry (optional)

Beat the egg whites in a mixing bowl until foamy. Add 1/4 cup sugar gradually, beating constantly until stiff peaks form. Scald the milk in a double boiler. Drop the meringue by tablespoonfuls over the milk. Poach gently for 4 minutes, turning the meringues once; do not allow the milk to boil. Remove the meringues to a tea towel using a slotted spoon and reserving the milk.

Beat the egg yolks in a mixing bowl just until blended. Beat in 1/4 cup sugar and the salt until smooth. Stir a small amount of the reserved warm milk mixture into the egg yolk mixture. Stir the egg yolk mixture into the reserved warm milk mixture. Cook until thickened, stirring frequently. Remove from the heat and stir in the vanilla. Cool slightly and pour the custard into a serving bowl. Arrange the meringues over the custard and chill until serving time.

Merry Draghi
Happy Chicken Farms/Merry Milk Maid
Urbancrest, Ohio

Panna Cotta
Serves 6

4 1/2 gelatin sheets
2 cups half-and-half
2 cups heavy cream
1 cup sugar
2 teaspoons cinnamon
1 1/2 teaspoons vanilla extract
1/4 teaspoon nutmeg

Bloom the gelatin in cold water in a bowl until soft. Combine the half-and-half, heavy cream, sugar, cinnamon, vanilla and nutmeg in a saucepan and bring just to a boil. Remove from the heat.

Remove the gelatin sheets from the water and stir into the cream mixture until smooth. Ladle the custard evenly into six 5-ounce custard cups. Chill for several hours or until set.

David Tetzloff
Executive Chef
G. Michael's Bistro
Columbus, Ohio

Buttermilk and Coconut Panna Cotta
Serves 6

1/2 cup buttermilk
1 1/2 teaspoons unflavored gelatin
2/3 cup heavy cream
3/4 cup sugar
1 1/2 cups buttermilk
1/2 cup shredded coconut

1 fresh pineapple, peeled
Rum to taste
6 scoops vanilla bean ice cream
6 slices angel food cake
Toasted coconut to taste

Mix 1/2 cup buttermilk and the gelatin in a bowl and let stand until softened. Combine the heavy cream and sugar in a saucepan and bring to a boil. Stir in the gelatin mixture, 1 1/2 cups buttermilk and 1/2 cup coconut. Ladle the custard into six 4-ounce ramekins and chill until set.

Slice the pineapple into six 1/4-inch slices. Grill the pineapple slices over hot coals or sear in a nonstick skillet for 1 1/2 minutes per side. Drizzle with rum while hot.

Scoop the ice cream and slightly flatten each scoop and refreeze.

To serve, dip the bottom of each ramekin into hot water for 30 seconds and invert each custard onto a dessert plate.

Stack 1 slice of the cake, 1 ice cream portion and 1 pineapple slice on each plate by the panna cotta and sprinkle toasted coconut over the pineapple. Serve immediately.

Russell Young
Executive Sous Chef
Hyatt on Capital Square
Columbus, Ohio

Brandied Tiramisù
Serves 4 to 6

10 to 12 ladyfingers
5 egg yolks
1/2 cup sugar
32 ounces mascarpone cheese
1/4 cup brandy
5 egg whites
1 cup espresso
Semisweet chocolate, shaved

Preheat the oven to 250 degrees. Arrange the ladyfingers in a single layer on a baking sheet and toast until dry and golden brown.

Beat the egg yolks and sugar in a mixing bowl until smooth and pale yellow. Add the cheese and brandy and beat until blended. Beat the egg whites in a mixing bowl until peaks form and fold into the cheese mixture. Dip the ladyfingers in the espresso.

Alternate layers of the ladyfingers and cheese mixture in a dish until all of the ingredients are used, ending with the cheese mixture. Sprinkle with shaved chocolate and chill, covered, for 24 hours.

If you are concerned about using raw eggs, use eggs pasteurized in their shells, which are sold at some specialty food stores, or use an equivalent amount of pasteurized egg substitute.

Simon Pesusich
Chef
Zia's
Toledo, Ohio

Tiramisù
Serves 4

2 ounces bittersweet chocolate, melted
5 egg yolks
2/3 cup sugar
16 ounces mascarpone cheese
5 egg whites

1/4 cup coffee
1 tablespoon espresso
1 tablespoon marsala
8 ladyfingers
1 ounce bittersweet chocolate, shaved

Fill a pastry bag with the melted chocolate and pipe the chocolate in a manner to line 4 martini glasses. Beat the egg yolks and sugar in a mixing bowl at high speed until light and pale yellow. Add the cheese and beat until combined. Beat the egg whites in a mixing bowl until medium to stiff peaks form. Fold the egg whites in 2 batches into the cheese mixture; do not overmix.

Mix the coffee, espresso and wine in a bowl. Break 1 ladyfinger into halves, dip in the espresso mixture and arrange in 1 of the prepared martini glasses.

Spoon 3 ounces of the cheese mixture over the ladyfinger. Break another ladyfinger into halves and dip in the espresso mixture. Arrange over the prepared layers and top with 3 more ounces of the cheese mixture. Sprinkle with some of the shaved chocolate. Repeat the process an additional 3 times with the remaining ladyfingers, remaining espresso mixture, remaining cheese mixture and remaining shaved chocolate. Chill for 1 to 2 hours before serving.

Octavio Reyes
Executive Chef
Martini's Italian Bistro
Columbus, Ohio

Apple Pastry

Apple Dumplings

Bananas Foster

Bananas Foster for One

Caramel Bananas

French Toast with Date Compote and Port Sauce

Cherry Strawberry Napoleon

Lemon Gratin with Lemon Cream

Fresh Peach Crisp

Berry Crisp

Rhubarb and Strawberry Crisp

Pear Pecan Crostini

Strawberry Pretzel Delight

Raspberry Truffles

fruit desserts

fruit desserts

Apple Pastry
Serves 24

APPLE FILLING
5 cups thinly sliced apples
2 cups sugar
1/2 cup ground walnuts
1/2 cup raisins (optional)
2 tablespoons sour cream

PASTRY AND ASSEMBLY
3/4 cup (1 1/2 sticks) butter, softened
3/4 cup sugar
1 egg, lightly beaten
1 teaspoon vanilla extract
Grated zest of 1 lemon
2 1/2 cups flour
1 teaspoon baking powder
Cinnamon to taste
Confectioners' sugar to taste

For the filling, combine the apples, sugar, walnuts, raisins and sour cream in a bowl and mix well.

For the pastry, preheat the oven to 350 degrees. Mix the butter and sugar in a bowl until creamy using a wooden spoon. Add the egg, vanilla and lemon zest and mix well.

Sift the flour and baking powder together and add a small amount of the flour mixture to the egg mixture. Turn the pastry onto a well floured hard surface and add the remaining flour mixture and mix well; the pastry will be stiff. Divide the pastry into 2 equal portions.

Roll 1 pastry portion into a rectangle and arrange in a 10×15-inch baking pan. Spread with the filling and sprinkle with cinnamon. Roll the remaining pastry portion into a rectangle and place on top of the filling. Prick the top of the pastry with a fork and bake for 1 hour. Cool for 15 minutes and cut into squares while warm. Sprinkle with confectioners' sugar and serve warm.

Amanda was a ProStart® student in Susan Serves' class at East High School. In addition to being a member of the Honor Roll and Merit Roll, Amanda received the Junior Ambassador Award, the Rotary Club Scholarship, and the 3.0 Club Award and was nominated to the National Honor Society. After acquiring skills in nutrition, culinary arts, and business management, Amanda would like to own her own hotel/restaurant chain.

Amanda Jones
East High School '04
Akron, Ohio

Apple Dumplings
Serves 6

SYRUP
2 cups cold water
1 1/2 cups sugar
1/4 teaspoon cinnamon
1/4 teaspoon nutmeg
1/4 cup (1/2 stick) margarine

DUMPLINGS
2 1/4 cups flour
2 teaspoons baking powder
1/2 teaspoon salt
2/3 cup shortening
1/2 cup milk
6 small apples, cored and peeled
1/3 cup sugar
1/4 teaspoon cinnamon
1/4 teaspoon nutmeg
Butter

For the syrup, mix the cold water, sugar, cinnamon and nutmeg in a saucepan and bring to a boil. Reduce the heat and simmer for 5 minutes, stirring occasionally. Stir in the margarine.

For the dumplings, preheat the oven to 375 degrees. Mix the flour, baking powder and salt in a bowl. Cut the shortening into the flour mixture until crumbly. Add the milk and stir just until the mixture adheres and forms a ball.

Roll the dough on a lightly floured surface and cut into 6 squares. Place 1 apple on each pastry square and sprinkle evenly with the sugar, cinnamon and nutmeg. Dot with butter. Moisten the edges of the squares and pinch the edges together to enclose the apple. Arrange the dumplings in a 9×13-inch baking pan and drizzle with the syrup. Bake for 45 minutes. Serve immediately.

Rochelle Schrecengost
Trumbull County JVS
Warren, Ohio

Bananas Foster
Serves 4

4 bananas
1/2 cup (1 stick) butter
1/4 cup packed brown sugar
1/4 cup rum
4 scoops French vanilla ice cream

Slice the bananas horizontally into halves. Sauté the bananas in the butter in a skillet for 3 minutes. Add the brown sugar and mix well. Stir in the rum and cook for 1 minute or until reduced, stirring constantly.

Place 1 scoop of ice cream in each of 4 dessert bowls. Top each scoop of ice cream with 2 banana halves and drizzle with some of the sauce. Serve immediately. The dessert may be flamed if desired.

Steve Frank
ProStart® Instructor
North High School
Akron, Ohio

Bananas Foster for One

Serves 1

1 tablespoon butter
1 tablespoon brown sugar
1/2 teaspoon cinnamon
1 banana, sliced
2 tablespoons Grand Marnier
2 scoops vanilla ice cream
Whipped cream
1 strawberry fan
Fresh mint leaves

Heat the butter, brown sugar and cinnamon in a skillet until the butter melts, stirring frequently. Stir in the banana and cook until the sauce is thickened and the mixture is heated through, stirring frequently. Add the liqueur and mix well. Ignite with a long match and allow the flames to subside.

Spoon the warm banana mixture over the ice cream in a dessert bowl. Top with a dollop of whipped cream, a strawberry fan and mint leaves. Serve immediately.

John "Bud" Moore II
Serenity Tea House
Coshocton, Ohio

Caramel Bananas

Serves 2 to 4

2 tablespoons butter
2 firm large bananas, cut lengthwise into halves
1 ounce brown sugar
2 tablespoons orange juice
2 tablespoons lemon juice
1/2 teaspoon cinnamon
1/2 ounce chopped walnuts

Heat the butter in a 12-inch nonstick sauté pan until melted. Sauté the banana halves in the butter until golden brown. Sprinkle with the brown sugar and cook until the mixture thickens slightly, stirring occasionally. Remove the bananas to dessert bowls using a slotted spoon and reserving the sauce.

Stir the orange juice, lemon juice and cinnamon into the reserved sauce and simmer until thickened, stirring frequently. Drizzle the sauce over the bananas and sprinkle with the walnuts. Serve immediately.

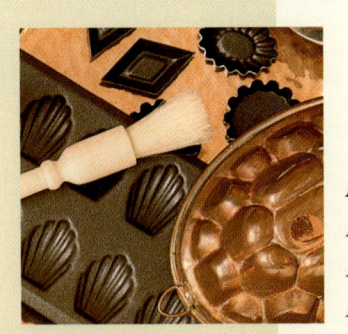

Kevin Tucky
Director of Special Events
Bucks Bar & Grill
Lexington, Ohio

French Toast with Date Compote and Port Sauce

Serves 2

PORT SAUCE
3/4 cup port

DATE COMPOTE
3 ounces sliced dates
2 ounces dried cherries
1/4 cup amaretto

FRENCH TOAST
1 egg
1 1/2 teaspoons sugar
1 1/2 teaspoons half-and-half
1/4 teaspoon allspice
2 slices French bread
Crème fraîche to taste
Mint leaves

For the sauce, heat the wine in a saucepan until reduced by 1/2. Pour into a covered container and chill until serving time.

For the compote, combine the dates, cherries and liqueur in a saucepan and mix well. Cook until all of the liquid is absorbed, stirring occasionally.

For the French toast, whisk the egg, sugar, half-and-half and allspice in a bowl until blended. Drizzle 1/2 of the sauce on each of 2 dessert plates and spoon 1/2 of the compote in the center of each plate. Dip the bread slices in the egg mixture and cook on a hot griddle until light brown on both sides. Arrange 1 warm bread slice over the compote on each plate and garnish with crème fraîche and mint leaves. Serve immediately.

Annette Lieb
EHOVE Career Center '05
Milan, Ohio

Cherry Strawberry Napoleon
Serves 4

Michael is in his tenth year as a culinary instructor, his fourth teaching ProStart®. In addition to an associate's degree in culinary arts and a bachelor's degree in food service management from Johnson and Wales, he will soon add Certified Secondary Foodservice Educator to his list of credentials. While he passes on the knowledge of twenty years of industry experience, Michael encourages his students to participate in FCCLA, Team Cuisine, and the Gordon Food Service Ohio ProStart® Student Competition. Michael supports the ProStart® program because it gives his students a head start on their careers through the National Certificate of Achievement.

1 1/4 cups flour
1/3 cup sugar
1/2 teaspoon baking powder
1/4 teaspoon baking soda
1/8 teaspoon salt
1/2 cup sour cream
2 tablespoons butter, softened

1 egg, lightly beaten
1 tablespoon vanilla extract
Whipped topping
Cherry Strawberry Topping (page 81)
Sugared Orange Zest (page 81)
4 edible yellow flowers

Preheat the oven to 350 degrees. Spray an 8-inch cake pan with nonstick cooking spray. Combine the flour, sugar, baking powder, baking soda and salt in a bowl and mix well. Combine the sour cream, butter, egg and vanilla in a bowl and mix until blended. Add the sour cream mixture to the flour mixture gradually, stirring constantly just until moistened.

Spread the batter in the prepared pan. Bake for 20 to 25 minutes or until a wooden pick inserted in the center comes out clean. Cool in the pan on a wire rack for at least 10 minutes.

To assemble, cut 4 rounds from the cake layer using a round cutter. Cut each round into 3 equal layers. Spread a small amount of whipped topping and some of the Cherry Strawberry Topping between each layer and stack on a dessert plate. Spoon the remaining Cherry Strawberry Topping over the top of each Napoleon until the topping begins to drizzle onto the plate. Pipe a small amount of whipped topping on the plate near the side of the dessert and sprinkle the Sugared Orange Zest over the whipped topping. Garnish with the edible flowers.

Michael Edwards
ProStart® Instructor
EHOVE Career Center
Milan, Ohio

Cherry Strawberry Topping
Makes 2 cups

1 cup canned tart cherries
1 cup sliced strawberries
5 tablespoons brown sugar
1 teaspoon sugar

Combine the cherries and strawberries in a bowl. Add the brown sugar and sugar and mix gently until the sugars dissolve and the fruit is coated.

Sugared Orange Zest
Serves 4

1 tablespoon grated orange zest
1 1/2 teaspoons sugar

Toss the orange zest and sugar in a bowl and spread the orange zest mixture on a sheet pan. Let stand at room temperature for 5 to 10 minutes.

Erik Goldstrom, a graduate of the Culinary Institute of America, joined Cameron Mitchell Restaurants in November of 1999 as a line cook. In early 2000, he became the Sous Chef at Mitchell's Steak House downtown and later that year moved into the Executive Chef's position at Cameron's Contemporary American Cuisine in Worthington. Erik's first experience with food came from his mother and grandmother. At home, Erik likes to cook pasta and grill out. Ironically, his favorite comfort food comes from a box: Hamburger Helper. He enjoys spectator sports, golfing, working in the yard, and fishing at his cabin in Sunbury, Ohio. He currently resides in German Village.

Lemon Gratin

Serves 6

32 ounces cream cheese, softened
1 3/4 cups sugar
Grated zest of 2 lemons
Grated zest of 1/2 orange
Juice of 2 lemons
Juice of 1/2 orange
3 egg yolks

1 1/2 teaspoons vanilla extract
3/4 cup whipping cream, whipped
2 teaspoons sour cream
3 egg whites, stiffly beaten
1 cup whipped cream
1 pint red raspberries
Lemon Cream (page 83)

Preheat the oven to 300 degrees. Spray six 10-ounce porcelain baking cups with nonstick cooking spray and coat with sugar. Arrange the cups in a baking pan. Beat the cream cheese, 1 3/4 cups sugar, the lemon zest and orange zest in a mixing bowl until creamy. Whisk the lemon juice, orange juice, egg yolks and vanilla in a bowl until blended and beat into the cream cheese mixture.

Fold in the whipped cream, sour cream and egg whites gently. Spoon 8 ounces of the cream cheese mixture into each prepared cup and smooth the surface. Add enough hot water to the baking pan to measure 1/2 inch.

Bake for 30 minutes and reduce the oven temperature to 225 degrees. Bake for 3 1/2 hours longer. The gratins should be slightly firm to the touch but not brown or cracked. Remove the cups from the baking pan and cool on a wire rack.

To serve, run a spatula around the outer edge of each gratin and invert onto dessert plates. Top each with a dollop of whipped cream and 3 or 4 raspberries. Serve immediately with Lemon Cream.

Erik Goldstrom
Executive Chef
Cameron's American Bistro
Worthington, Ohio

Lemon Cream

Makes 1 cup

1 cup half-and-half
Juice and zest of 1 lemon
1/2 cup sugar
3 egg yolks

Combine the half-and-half, lemon juice and lemon zest in a saucepan and mix well. Heat the half-and-half mixture just until bubbles appear around the edge of the pan and remove from the heat. Mix the sugar and eggs yolks in a bowl until the sugar dissolves.

Stir the egg yolk mixture into the half-and-half mixture and cook over low heat just until the sauce begins to thicken, stirring frequently. Remove from the heat and place the saucepan in a bowl of ice water. Let stand until cool, stirring occasionally.

Fresh Peach Crisp
Serves 10

1 cup sifted flour
1 cup sugar
1/2 teaspoon cinnamon
1/4 teaspoon salt
1/2 cup (1 stick) butter, softened
2 1/2 pounds peaches, peeled and sliced
Whipped cream

Preheat the oven to 375 degrees. Sift the flour, sugar, cinnamon and salt into a bowl and mix well. Cut the butter into the flour mixture until crumbly.

Arrange the peaches in a greased 8×8-inch baking dish and sprinkle with the crumb mixture. Bake for 45 to 50 minutes or until brown and bubbly. Serve warm topped with whipped cream.

Jay was a ProStart® student at Kettering Fairmont High School Career Tech Center and a member of their Knowledge Bowl Team for the 2004 Gordon Food Service Ohio ProStart® Student Competition. He really enjoyed the competition and meeting other students as well as visiting the exhibits at the North American Pizza and Ice Cream Show. His future plans include degrees in business management and culinary arts with a goal of opening his own restaurant.

Jay Williams
Kettering Fairmont High School
Career Tech Center '04
Kettering, Ohio

Berry Crisp
Serves 17

CRISP
1 1/2 pounds frozen raspberries
1 1/2 pounds frozen blueberries
1 1/2 pounds frozen blackberries
1 1/2 pounds frozen strawberries
1 1/4 cups sugar
1/2 cup kirsch
1 1/4 cups cornstarch
1 1/4 cups water

OAT TOPPING
2 cups flour
2 cups quick-cooking oats
1 (1-pound) package brown sugar
1/2 teaspoon cinnamon
1 cup (2 sticks) butter, softened

For the crisp, thaw the frozen berries in the refrigerator for 8 to 10 hours; drain, reserving the juice. Combine the reserved juice, sugar and brandy in a saucepan and mix well. Bring to a boil and stir in a mixture of the cornstarch and water. Cook until bright red in color and thickened, stirring frequently. Add the thickened juice mixture to the berries in a bowl and mix gently. Spoon the berry mixture into ramekins sprayed with nonstick cooking spray.

For the topping, preheat a convection oven to 375 degrees. Mix the flour, oats, brown sugar and cinnamon in a bowl. Cut the butter into the flour mixture until crumbly. Sprinkle approximately 1/3 cup of the crumb mixture over each ramekin and bake for 15 minutes or until bubbly. Serve immediately topped with vanilla ice cream.

Sean Schmidt
Chef
Parkers Blue Ash Grill
Blue Ash, Ohio

Rhubarb and Strawberry Crisp
Serves 6

1 (16-ounce) package frozen rhubarb, thawed
1 (16-ounce) package frozen strawberries, thawed
1/4 cup sugar
2 teaspoons flour
1 teaspoon grated lemon zest
2 1/2 cups oat granola

Preheat the oven to 350 degrees. Combine the undrained rhubarb, undrained strawberries, sugar, flour and lemon zest in a bowl and mix well. Spoon the rhubarb mixture into a buttered 9×13-inch baking dish and sprinkle with the granola. Bake until brown and bubbly. Serve warm.

Jim brings twenty-six years of culinary expertise to his position at Columbus State Community College. In addition to being a Fellow of the American Academy of Chefs and a member of the Honor Society of the American Culinary Federation, Jim has twice been named Chef of the Year by the Columbus Chapter of the ACF. Jim coordinated Ohio's pilot program for ProStart®. Now, he gets to work firsthand with ProStart® students as he moderates the Knowledge Bowl at the Gordon Food Service Ohio ProStart® Student Competition and as the graduates of the ProStart® program attend Columbus State Community College.

Jim Taylor, CEC, AAC
Hospitality Management Department
Columbus State Community College

Pear Pecan Crostini
Serves 10 to 12

10 ounces blue cheese (Roquefort, Gorgonzola or Stilton)
5 tablespoons heavy cream
15 slices Panera Cinnamon Raisin bread, crusts trimmed
2 Bartlett pears
1/3 cup pecan halves, thinly sliced crosswise

Preheat the oven to 350 degrees. Mix the cheese and heavy cream in a bowl until of a spreading consistency using a fork or wooden spoon.

Cut the bread into 1 1/2-inch squares and arrange in a single layer on a baking sheet. Toast for 6 minutes on each side or until light brown.

Cut the pears into thin wedges approximately 1 1/2 inches long. Spread 1 heaping teaspoon of the cheese mixture on each crostini and top each with a pear wedge and pecan slice. Serve at room temperature.

Panera Bread
Breads of the World
Columbus, Ohio

Strawberry Pretzel Delight

Serves 15

PRETZEL CRUST
2 cups crushed pretzels
3/4 cup (1 1/2 sticks) margarine
1 tablespoon sugar

CREAM CHEESE FILLING
8 ounces cream cheese, softened
8 ounces whipped topping
1 cup sugar

STRAWBERRY TOPPING
1 (6-ounce) package strawberry gelatin
2 cups boiling water
2 (10-ounce) packages frozen strawberries

For the crust, preheat the oven to 400 degrees. Combine the crushed pretzels, margarine and sugar in a bowl and mix well. Press over a 9×13-inch baking pan. Bake for 8 minutes; do not overbake. Let stand until cool.

For the filling, beat the cream cheese, whipped topping and sugar in a mixing bowl until creamy, scraping the bowl occasionally. Spread the cream cheese mixture over the baked layer. Chill for 20 minutes.

For the topping, dissolve the gelatin in the boiling water in a heatproof bowl. Stir in the frozen strawberries. Let stand until partially set and spread the strawberry mixture over the prepared layers. Chill until set.

With over sixty-two years of baking experience, Dee purchased the Derr Road Inn so she could share with the general public all the dessert recipes that family and friends have enjoyed for years. Regions Business Magazine has named Derr Road Inn "Springfield's Best Fine Dining Restaurant" for over seven years in a row.

Dee Klosterman
Klosterman's Derr Road Inn
Springfield, Ohio

Raspberry Truffles
Makes 2 dozen

2 cups heavy cream
1 1/2 pounds semisweet chocolate, coarsely chopped
2 tablespoons Chambord
Baking cocoa or crushed nuts

Bring the heavy cream to a boil in a saucepan. Remove from the heat and whisk in the chocolate until blended. Stir in the liqueur. Chill until firm.

Shape the chocolate mixture into 1-inch balls and coat with baking cocoa or crushed nuts. Chill until firm.

Karen Bennett
Pastry Chef
LACENTRE Conference-Banquet Facility
Westlake, Ohio

Apple Pie with a Squeeze

Apple Walnut Pie

Brown Bag Apple Pie

Orchard-to-Table Apple Pie

Upside-Down Banana Cream Pie with Pale Ale Caramel Sauce and Candied Pecans

Coconut Cream Pies with Cookie Pie Pastries

Chocolate Silk Pies

French Silk Pie

Chocolate Fudge Pie

Key Lime Pies

Lemon Sour Cream Pie

Peanut Butter Pie

Pecan Pies

Shark Fin Pie

Vinegar Pie

Warm Apple Tarts with Rosemary

Chocolate Tarts with White Chocolate Mousse

Pecan Tassies

Lemon Gingersnap Tart

Danish Puff

Tosca Cups

fries tarts pastries

Apple Pie with a Squeeze
Serves 6 to 8

Tyler was a ProStart® student at Lorain County JVS and captain of the culinary team that won the gold medal at the 2004 Gordon Food Service Ohio ProStart® Competition. While in school, Tyler commuted to Mansfield on weekends to work at Skyway East Restaurant and Westbrook Country Club. He was also active in FCCLA, Team Cuisine, and Junior American Culinary Federation. As a scholar athlete with a varsity letter in golf, he still managed to find time to do volunteer work in the community. After completing his education at the Culinary Institute of America, his goal is to become a certified master chef.

1 teaspoon cinnamon
3/4 cup raw sugar
1/4 cup flour
1/4 cup golden raisins
2 cups water
2 tablespoons lemon juice
1 1/2 pounds Granny Smith apples, peeled and cut into 1/4-inch slices

Cheddar Cheese Pastry (page 93)
1 teaspoon butter, melted
1 egg, beaten
2 teaspoons water
1 tablespoon raw sugar

Toast the cinnamon in a small sauté pan over high heat until aromatic. Shock the pan in an ice bath. Combine the cinnamon, 3/4 cup sugar, the flour and raisins in a bowl and mix well. Mix 2 cups water and the lemon juice in a bowl. Add the apples to the lemon juice mixture and toss to coat; drain.

Preheat the oven to 425 degrees. Divide the pastry into 2 equal portions. Roll 1 dough portion 1/4 inch thick on a lightly floured surface and fit into a 9-inch pie plate. Brush the bottom of the pie shell with the butter to keep the crust from getting soggy. Layer the apples and raisin mixture in the pie shell.

Roll the remaining dough portion 1/4 inch thick on a lightly floured surface. Cut into 3/4-inch strips. Moisten the edge of the bottom pastry with water. Arrange the strips lattice-fashion over the apple mixture. Seal the edges, turn under the excess and crimp. Cut apple cutouts from the dough scraps to decorate the top of the pie.

Whisk the egg and 2 teaspoons water in a bowl until blended and brush over the lattice top. Sprinkle with 1 tablespoon sugar. Bake for 15 minutes and reduce the oven temperature to 350 degrees. Bake for 45 minutes longer. Let stand until cool and serve.

Tyler K. Mock
Lorain County JVS '04
Oberlin, Ohio

Cheddar Cheese Pastry
Makes 2

2 ounces Cheddar cheese
1/2 teaspoon nutmeg
2 cups flour
1/2 teaspoon salt
3/4 cup shortening
1/4 cup (1/2 stick) butter, chilled and cut into 1/8-inch pieces
1/2 cup ice water

Shred the cheese finely. For best results, shred the cheese 1 day in advance and store, covered, in the refrigerator to remove some of the moisture. Toast the nutmeg in a sauté pan over high heat until aromatic and then shock the pan in an ice bath.

Combine the cheese, nutmeg, flour and salt in a bowl and mix well. Cut in the shortening and butter until crumbly. Add the ice water 1 tablespoon at a time until the flour mixture is moistened; do not overmix. Shape the pastry into a ball.

Apple Walnut Pie
Serves 10

WALNUT TOPPING
5 tablespoons butter
3 ounces brown sugar
1/2 cup chopped walnuts

PASTRY
1 1/3 cups flour
1/2 teaspoon salt
1/2 cup shortening
3 tablespoons cold water

APPLE FILLING
1 1/2 cups sugar
1/4 cup flour
1 teaspoon nutmeg
1 teaspoon cinnamon
1/4 teaspoon salt
8 apples, peeled and chopped

For the topping, heat the butter in a saucepan until melted and cool slightly. Place the brown sugar in a mixing bowl and pour the butter over the brown sugar gradually, beating constantly at medium speed. Beat for 2 to 4 minutes longer. Spread the brown sugar mixture over the bottom of a 10-inch pie plate and sprinkle with the walnuts.

For the pastry, combine the flour and salt in a bowl and cut in the shortening until crumbly using 2 forks. Add the cold water 1 tablespoon at a time and mix until the mixture forms a ball.

Divide the pastry into 2 portions and roll each portion on a lightly floured surface into a circle. Arrange 1 circle over the topping.

For the filling, preheat the oven to 350 degrees. Combine the sugar, flour, nutmeg, cinnamon and salt in a saucepan and mix well. Stir in the apples and cook until heated through, stirring occasionally. Spoon the apple mixture into the prepared pie plate and top with the remaining pastry circle.

Bake the pie for 1 hour. Let stand until cool and invert onto a serving plate. Serve with whipped cream and/or ice cream.

Curtis Parker
Chef
John Q's Steakhouse
Cleveland, Ohio

Brown Bag Apple Pie
Serves 6

8 cups chopped peeled apples
1/2 cup sugar
1 tablespoon flour
1 teaspoon cinnamon
1 unbaked (9- or 10-inch) pie shell
1/2 cup sugar
1/2 cup flour
1/2 cup (1 stick) margarine

Preheat the oven to 400 degrees. Combine the apples, 1/2 cup sugar, 1 tablespoon flour and the cinnamon in a bowl and mix well. Mound the apple mixture in the pie shell. Mix 1/2 cup sugar and 1/2 cup flour in a bowl and cut in the margarine until crumbly. Pat the crumb mixture over the apples to cover.

Place the pie in a brown paper bag that does not include recycled material and fold the end to seal. Bake for 1 hour. Remove the pie from the bag and let stand on a wire rack until cool.

Ida Mast
Kitchen Manager
The Amish Door Restaurant
Wilmot, Ohio

Orchard-to-Table Apple Pie
Serves 8

Greg was a ProStart® student at Lorain County JVS and a member of the management team that took first place at both the 2003 and 2004 Gordon Food Service Ohio ProStart® Student Competition and the 2003 and 2004 National ProStart® Student Invitational. While working at Viscaya Italian Restaurant, Nemo Grille, and Giant Eagle Corporation as well as running his own catering company, Chef-to-Be, Greg also found time to compete at FCCLA and Team Cuisine. After completing his education at the Culinary Institute of America, Greg wants to obtain a rewarding position in the food service industry.

1/2 cup packed brown sugar
3 tablespoons cornstarch
1 teaspoon cinnamon
1 teaspoon vanilla extract
8 to 10 assorted apples, such as McIntosh, Granny Smith and/or Fugi (about 4 pounds)
1 tablespoon lemon juice
1/2 teaspoon nutmeg
Apple Pie Pastry (page 97)
1 egg white, beaten, or melted butter
2 tablespoons butter, chilled

Mix the brown sugar, cornstarch, cinnamon and vanilla in a bowl. Peel and slice the apples and toss with the lemon juice in a bowl. Add the brown sugar mixture to the apples and mix gently.

Preheat the oven to 425 degrees. Roll each of the pastry portions into an 11-inch round on a lightly floured and sugared hard surface. Do not press hard with the rolling pin; allow it to roll with minimum pressure. Roll from the center out, lifting and turning to avoid sticking, with a lightly floured rolling pin. If the pastry tears, just moisten the edges of the seam and roll lightly. Do not shape into a ball and reroll.

Gently loosen 1 of the pastry rounds with a metal spatula and fold the pastry over to form a semicircle. Slide the folded pastry into a 9-inch pie plate and unfold.

Press the dough gently into the pie plate and brush the bottom with some of the egg white.

Spoon the apple mixture into the pastry-lined pie plate and dot with the butter. Fold the remaining pastry round in half and cut several slits in the pastry. Gently transfer to the top of the pie and unfold. Trim the pastry, allowing a 1-inch overhang, and press the pastry on the apple filling. Tuck the overhang under the bottom crust and seal the edge by pinching, using a fork or twisting the edge. Use the trimmings of the pastry to create cutouts of your choice to decorate the top of the pie. Brush with the remaining egg white.

Place the pie on a baking sheet lined with foil. Bake for 40 to 50 minutes or until the juice bubbles through the slits and the pastry is golden brown. Cool on a wire rack. You may serve with natural vanilla bean ice cream, caramel sauce and a mint leaf if desired.

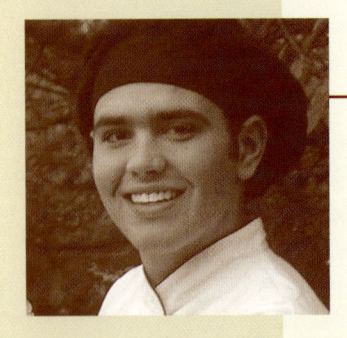

Gregory N. Mezey
Lorain County JVS '04
Oberlin, Ohio

Apple Pie Pastry
Makes 2

- 3 cups all-purpose flour
- 1 cup cake flour
- 1 cup shortening, chilled and cut into pieces
- 1 cup (2 sticks) unsalted butter, chilled and cut into pieces
- 1 teaspoon salt
- 1/2 cup ice water
- 1 egg, beaten
- 1 tablespoon vinegar

Mix the all-purpose flour, cake flour, shortening, butter and salt in a bowl with a pastry blender until crumbly; some larger chunks of butter and shortening will be visible. Do not overwork the dough as this can cause a tough and less flaky pastry. Avoid using your fingers to mix because it melts the butter and shortening and does not allow small chunks to remain. The small chunks disperse through the dough when the pastry bakes.

Whisk the ice water, egg and vinegar in a bowl until blended. Add the egg mixture to the crumb mixture gradually, stirring constantly with a fork until the flour is completely mixed in but does not form a ball. Shape the dough into 2 equal discs; small butter chunks should be visible. Chill, covered with plastic wrap, for 2 hours. Let the dough sit at room temperature for 10 minutes before rolling.

Upside-Down Banana Cream Pie
Serves 6

GRAHAM CRACKER CRUST
1 1/4 cups graham cracker crumbs
1 cup (1/2-inch) pieces graham crackers
6 1/2 tablespoons butter, melted
2 tablespoons sugar

PIE
3 cups half-and-half
1 teaspoon unflavored gelatin
1/2 cup sugar
2 tablespoons butter
1/16 teaspoon salt
3 tablespoons cornstarch
2 egg yolks, lightly beaten
3 tablespoons banana liqueur
1/2 vanilla bean, split
12 bananas, sliced
Whipped cream
Pale Ale Caramel Sauce (page 99)
Candied Pecans (page 99)

For the crust, combine the graham cracker crumbs, graham cracker pieces, butter and sugar in a bowl and mix well.

For the pie, mix 2 cups of the half-and-half and the gelatin in a double boiler and let stand for 3 to 5 minutes or until softened. Stir in the sugar, butter and salt. Bring to a boil, stirring constantly. Whisk the remaining 1 cup half-and-half, cornstarch, egg yolks, liqueur and vanilla bean in a bowl until combined.

Add the egg yolk mixture to the gelatin mixture gradually, stirring constantly. Cook until thickened, stirring constantly. Strain into a bowl, discarding the solids. Chill in an ice bath, stirring occasionally.

To assemble, layer 1/3 cup of the crust, 1/2 cup of the custard, 1/2 of a banana and whipped cream in each of 6 dessert bowls. Drizzle each with some of the Pale Ale Caramel Sauce and sprinkle each with 2 tablespoons of the Candied Pecans. Serve immediately.

Mike Bell
Executive Chef
Columbus Brewing Company
Columbus, Ohio

Pale Ale Caramel Sauce
Makes 2 cups

1 3/4 cups sugar
1 cup plus 2 tablespoons corn syrup
14 tablespoons butter
1 cup heavy cream, heated
1 cup Columbus pale ale

Combine the sugar and corn syrup in a saucepan and mix well. Cook over medium heat until the mixture is amber in color, stirring occasionally. Remove from the heat and add the butter, heavy cream and ale, stirring until smooth.

Candied Pecans
Makes 1/2 cup

1/2 cup chopped pecans
1 tablespoon water
1 tablespoon sugar
1/8 teaspoon cinnamon

Preheat the oven to 400 degrees. Spread the pecans in a single layer on a baking sheet and toast the pecans until hot. Remove the pecans to a stainless steel bowl and sprinkle with the water. Add the sugar and cinnamon and toss to coat.

Return the pecans to the baking sheet and toast until crisp; watch carefully to prevent overbrowning. Remove to a plate to cool.

Coconut Cream Pies
Makes 2

2 (4-ounce) packages vanilla pudding and pie filling mix
1/2 cup shredded coconut
1/4 cup blanched slivered almonds
1 cup frozen whipped topping, thawed
3 tablespoons coconut flavoring
Frozen whipped topping to taste, thawed
Cookie Pie Pastries (page 101)

Prepare the pudding mixes using the package directions. Chill, covered, for 2 to 10 hours.

Preheat the oven to 350 degrees. Spread the coconut on a baking sheet and toast just until the coconut begins to turn golden brown. Remove to a platter to cool. Spread the almonds on a baking sheet and toast for 3 to 4 minutes or until crisp but have not changed color. Remove to a platter to cool.

Beat the pudding in a mixing bowl until smooth and fluffy. Fold in 1 cup whipped topping and the flavoring. Fold in the coconut and almonds. Spoon the filling evenly into the 2 baked pie shells. Swirl additional whipped topping to taste over the top and sprinkle with additional toasted coconut and toasted almonds if desired. Chill until serving time.

John and Kathy Babas
Waterloo Restaurant
Akron, Ohio

Cookie Pie Pastries
Makes 2

2 cups flour
1/4 cup sugar
1 teaspoon salt
3/4 cup lard, chilled and cut into pieces
2 tablespoons butter, chilled and cut into pieces
1/4 cup milk
1 egg

Preheat the oven to 450 degrees. Combine the flour, sugar and salt in a bowl and mix well. Cut in the lard and butter with a pastry blender until crumbly. Whisk the milk and egg in a bowl until blended and drizzle over the flour mixture, stirring with a fork. Shape the dough into a ball and knead briefly. Chill, wrapped with plastic wrap, for at least 30 minutes.

Divide the dough into 2 equal portions. Roll each portion into a 12-inch round on a well floured hard surface and fit each round into a 9-inch pie plate. Crimp the edges and prick the sides and bottoms at 1-inch intervals with a fork. Bake for 20 minutes or until the centers are brown. Cool completely before filling.

Chocolate Silk Pies
Makes 2

PECAN CRUST
2 cups pecans
2 cups graham cracker crumbs
2/3 cup packed dark brown sugar
1/2 cup (1 stick) butter, melted

CHOCOLATE FILLING
12 eggs, at room temperature
1 1/2 teaspoons vanilla extract
12 ounces semisweet chocolate, coarsely chopped
10 ounces unsweetened chocolate, coarsely chopped
2 1/4 cups whipping cream
3 tablespoons sugar

For the crust, preheat the oven to 350 degrees. Spread the pecans in a single layer on a baking sheet and toast for 7 to 8 minutes, stirring occasionally. Remove to a platter to cool. Maintain the oven temperature.

Line the bottom of two 9-inch springform pans with baking parchment and spray the baking parchment and the sides of the pans generously with nonstick cooking spray. Process the pecans in a blender until medium ground. Combine the pecans, graham cracker crumbs, brown sugar and butter in a bowl and mix well. Press the pecan mixture evenly over the bottoms of the prepared pans. Bake for 13 to 15 minutes or until light brown. Let stand until cool.

For the filling, whisk the eggs and vanilla in a bowl until blended. Heat the semisweet chocolate and unsweetened chocolate in a double boiler until blended, stirring occasionally. Remove from the heat and whisk in the egg mixture. Pour the chocolate mixture into a bowl and let cool for 5 minutes.

Beat the whipping cream and sugar in a mixing bowl at medium-high speed until peaks form. Fold the whipped cream into the chocolate mixture until smooth. Spoon about 4 cups of the chocolate filling into each prepared pan. Chill for 24 hours.

If concerned about using raw eggs, use eggs pasteurized in their shells or an equivalent amount of pasteurized egg substitute.

Peter and Laurie Danis
Figlio
Columbus, Ohio

French Silk Pie

Makes 2

2 cups chocolate sandwich cookie crumbs
3 cups heavy cream
1 cup sugar
16 egg yolks, lightly beaten
20 ounces semisweet chocolate, coarsely chopped
2 teaspoons vanilla extract
Whipped cream
Chocolate curls

Press the cookie crumbs into two 9-inch pie plates. Combine the heavy cream and sugar in a double boiler and heat until the cream mixture is hot and bubbles form around the edge of the pan, stirring occasionally. Stir 1/4 of the hot cream mixture into the egg yolks. Stir the egg yolks into the hot cream mixture.

Cook over high heat until thickened and the consistency of a custard, whisking constantly. Remove from the heat and stir in the chocolate until blended. Stir in the vanilla.

Spoon the chocolate mixture evenly into the prepared pie plates. Press plastic wrap directly onto the surface of the filling and chill for 4 to 10 hours. Garnish with whipped cream and chocolate curls.

Dianne Piccinino
Chef
The Clarmont Restaurant
Columbus, Ohio

Chocolate Fudge Pie
Serves 8

1 cup (2 sticks) unsalted butter
6 ounces semisweet chocolate, coarsely chopped
9 eggs, lightly beaten
1 1/2 cups sugar
1 teaspoon vanilla extract
1/8 teaspoon salt
1 unbaked (10-inch) pie shell

Preheat the oven to 300 degrees. Heat the butter and chocolate in a double boiler until blended, stirring frequently. Pour the chocolate mixture into a heatproof bowl and cool slightly. Add the eggs, sugar, vanilla and salt to the chocolate mixture and whisk until smooth.

Spoon the chocolate mixture into the pie shell and bake for 40 to 45 minutes or until the center is almost set. Let stand until cool. The filling will firm up as it cools. Serve with whipped cream or topping.

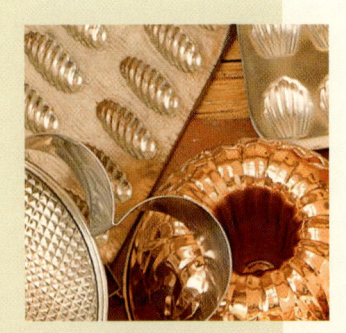

Denise Denman
Chef
Shaw's Restaurant & Inn
Lancaster, Ohio

Key Lime Pies
Makes 2

GRAHAM CRACKER CRUST
4 cups graham cracker crumbs
1/2 cup sugar
1/2 cup (1 stick) butter, melted

KEY LIME FILLING
3 (14-ounce) cans sweetened condensed milk
2 cups fresh Key lime juice
6 egg yolks, lightly beaten

TOPPING
4 cups whipping cream
4 ounces confectioners' sugar

For the crust, preheat the oven to 325 degrees. Combine the graham cracker crumbs, sugar and butter in a bowl and mix well. Press the crumb mixture over the bottoms and up the sides of two 10-inch pie plates. Bake for 15 minutes. Reduce the oven temperature to 300 degrees.

For the filling, combine the condensed milk, lime juice and egg yolks in a bowl and mix well. Pour the filling evenly into the two prepared pie plates. Bake for 20 minutes. Let stand until cool.

For the topping, beat the whipping cream and confectioners' sugar in a mixing bowl until stiff peaks form. Pipe the whipped cream over the filling and chill until serving time.

Justin Whites
Chef
Jay's Restaurant
Dayton, Ohio

Lemon Sour Cream Pie
Serves 6 to 8

1 1/2 cups sugar
7 tablespoons cornstarch
1/8 teaspoon salt
1 1/2 cups water
3 egg yolks, beaten
2 tablespoons butter
1 teaspoon grated lemon zest
1/2 cup lemon juice
1 cup sour cream
1 baked (9-inch) vanilla wafer pie shell

Combine the sugar, cornstarch and salt in a saucepan and mix well. Stir in the water and bring to a boil over medium heat. Cook for 5 minutes or until thickened, stirring frequently. Remove from the heat. Stir a small amount of the hot mixture into the egg yolks. Stir the egg yolks into the hot mixture.

Bring to a boil and boil for 1 minute, stirring constantly. Remove from the heat. Stir in the butter and lemon zest. Add the lemon juice gradually, stirring constantly. Cool to lukewarm, stirring frequently to prevent a film from forming. Stir in the sour cream. Spoon the lemon mixture into the pie shell. Chill until set.

As a graduate of Michigan State University with a bachelor's degree in food service management, Jay brings forty-four years of experience to Jay's Restaurant in Dayton's Oregon District. In addition to being a past chairman of the Ohio Restaurant Association, Jay has served on numerous committees as well as being a past president of the Miami Valley Restaurant Association. Jay believes in the benefits of ProStart® and has served on Advisory Boards, given students internships, and mentored a teacher. Jay gives his time, talents, and resources for the future of the industry.

Jay Haverstick
Jay's Restaurant
Dayton, Ohio

Peanut Butter Pie
Serves 6 to 8

10 ounces cream cheese
1 1/2 cups peanut butter
1 1/4 cups confectioners' sugar
3/4 cup milk
1/2 cup whipped cream
1 (9-inch) graham cracker pie shell
Chocolate syrup (optional)
Whipped cream (optional)
Fresh strawberry fans (optional)
Cinnamon (optional)

Beat the cream cheese in a mixing bowl for 4 minutes or until creamy. Add the peanut butter, confectioners' sugar and milk and beat until smooth, scraping the bowl occasionally. Fold in 1/2 cup whipped cream. Spoon the peanut butter filling into the pie shell.

Chill for 2 1/2 hours or until firm. Slice the pie and garnish each serving with chocolate syrup, additional whipped cream, 2 strawberry fans and a sprinkle of cinnamon.

Dewayne Gault
Invention Family Restaurant
Milan, Ohio

Pecan Pies
Makes 2 pies

3 1/4 cups sugar
2 cups light corn syrup
4 1/2 tablespoons butter
9 eggs
1/4 cup vanilla extract
2 unbaked (9-inch) Cookie Pie Pastries (page 101)
2 cups pecan halves

Combine the sugar, corn syrup and butter in a saucepan and cook over medium heat until the sugar dissolves, stirring frequently. Chill, covered, for 8 to 10 hours. Bring the syrup mixture to room temperature.

Preheat the oven to 350 degrees. Beat the eggs and vanilla in a mixing bowl until thick but not fluffy. Add the syrup mixture to the egg mixture and mix well. Pour evenly into the Cookie Pie Pastries.

Bake for 20 to 25 minutes or until the edges of the filling begin to bubble. Sprinkle 1 cup of the pecans over each pie.

Bake for 25 to 30 minutes longer or until the center is almost set but still trembles slightly when lightly shaken. Let stand until cool. The filling becomes firmer as it cools.

When John and Kathy took over the restaurant in 1957, they made pies their specialty. On the strength of apple, pecan, and coconut cream, the restaurant grew from a drive-in to 200 seats and spawned a thriving catering business.

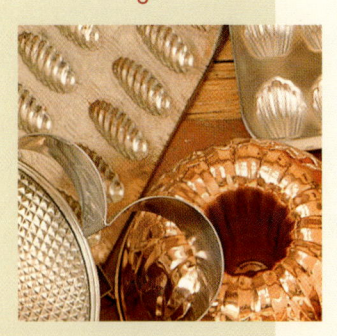

John and Kathy Babas
Waterloo Restaurant
Akron, Ohio

Shark Fin Pie

Serves 8

CHOCOLATE COOKIE CRUMB CRUST
1 3/4 cups chocolate sandwich cookie crumbs
1/4 cup (1/2 stick) butter, melted

CHOCOLATE ICE CREAM FILLING AND ASSEMBLY
1 gallon Butter Fudge Ripple ice cream, slightly softened
1/2 cup peanut butter
1/2 cup fudge sauce
2 cups ground honey-roasted peanuts
Chocolate syrup
Whipped cream
Chopped honey-roasted peanuts

For the crust, preheat the oven to 300 degrees. Combine the cookie crumbs and butter in a bowl and mix well. Press the crumb mixture into two 10-inch metal pie plates. Bake for 6 to 8 minutes. Let stand until cool and freeze.

For the filling, spoon enough of the ice cream into the pie shells to reach to the top edge of the pie plates. Spread the peanut butter over the ice cream and then spread with the fudge sauce. Sprinkle with 1/2 cup of the ground peanuts. Freeze until firm.

Mound the remaining ice cream over the top of the prepared layers and freeze until firm. Sprinkle with the remaining 1 1/2 cups ground peanuts. Serve garnished with chocolate syrup, whipped cream and chopped honey-roasted peanuts.

Kevin Jones
Executive Chef
Mitchell's Fish Market
Columbus, Ohio

Vinegar Pie
Serves 8

VINEGAR PIE PASTRY
5 ounces flour
1 1/2 teaspoons sugar
1/2 teaspoon salt
3 ounces shortening, chilled
2 tablespoons milk
1 1/2 teaspoons vinegar
1/2 egg yolk

VINEGAR FILLING
12 ounces sugar
1/2 cup (1 stick) butter, melted
2 eggs, lightly beaten
3 1/2 teaspoons vinegar
3 1/2 teaspoons vanilla extract

For the pastry, sift the flour, sugar and salt into a bowl and mix well. Cut the shortening into the flour mixture until crumbly. Whisk the milk, vinegar and egg yolk in a bowl until blended and toss with the flour mixture just until moistened. Shape the pastry into a disc and chill, wrapped in plastic wrap, for 30 minutes.

Roll the pastry into a 12-inch round on a lightly floured surface. Fit the pastry round into a 9-inch pie plate and trim and flute the edge.

For the filling, preheat the oven to 350 degrees. Combine the sugar and butter in a bowl and stir until the sugar dissolves. Add the eggs, vinegar and vanilla and stir gently to prevent the formation of excess foam.

Pour the vinegar filling into the pastry-lined pie plate. Bake for 50 minutes or until a knife inserted 2/3 of the distance to the center comes out clean.

Deane Cobler
Culinary Instructor
Columbus State Community College
Columbus, Ohio

Warm Apple Tarts with Rosemary

Serves 4

10 ounces frozen puff pastry, thawed
1 Golden Delicious apple or
 Anjou pear
1/3 cup sugar
1/4 cup (1/2 stick) unsalted butter
2 tablespoons sugar
1/2 teaspoon finely chopped
 fresh rosemary

4 Golden Delicious apples or
 Anjou pears
1/4 cup (1/2 stick) unsalted butter
2 tablespoons sugar
3 tablespoons sifted confectioners' sugar
4 sprigs of fresh mint

Roll the puff pastry 1/2 inch thick on a lightly floured surface. Cut out four 5-inch rounds using a cutter. Arrange the rounds on a baking sheet lined with baking parchment or waxed paper. Chill for 25 minutes or longer.

Peel and finely chop 1 apple. Combine the chopped apple, 1/3 cup sugar and 1/4 cup butter in a saucepan and cook over low heat until the apple is very soft, the sugar dissolves and the mixture is of a spreading consistency, stirring frequently. Let stand until cool.

Preheat the oven to 350 degrees. Cut four 6-inch squares of baking parchment or waxed paper and arrange the squares on a baking sheet. Sprinkle the sheets evenly with 2 tablespoons sugar.

Place the pastry rounds on top of the sugar and prick the entire surface of the pastry with a fork. Spread each with 1 tablespoon of the apple mixture and sprinkle with the rosemary. Peel and thinly slice 4 apples. Fan the apple slices in a circular pattern over the rosemary.

Heat 1/4 cup butter in a saucepan and coat the tops of the tarts with the butter. Sprinkle with 2 tablespoons sugar. Bake for 18 minutes or until the apples begin to caramelize and turn light brown. Serve warm dusted with the confectioners' sugar and topped with the sprigs of fresh mint.

Chef Richard Blondin
Chef de Cuisine
The Refectory
Columbus, Ohio

Chocolate Tarts with White Chocolate Mousse
Serves 20

What began as a summer job at seventeen has grown into a full-fledged career and never-ending passion for Stephanie. After graduating from the Culinary Institute of America, she honed her skills at hotels and high cuisine beach resorts before an opportunity came to expand her pastry skills working for Sodexho. Finally, Stephanie came to Longaberger, where she directs food preparations for events ranging from small private executive luncheons to events for 3,000 people. As a judge for the Gordon Food Service Ohio ProStart® Student Competition, Stephanie shares her expertise and helps to educate future chefs.

1 pound flour
11 ounces baking cocoa
2 1/4 cups (4 1/2 sticks) butter, softened
9 ounces sugar
2 eggs
1/16 teaspoon salt
1/4 cup cold water
18 ounce white chocolate, chopped

3/4 cup milk, heated
5 cups whipping cream
18 ounces vanilla yogurt
1/2 ounce unflavored gelatin
1/3 cup water
Fresh raspberries
Raspberry Sauce (page 113)
Vanilla Rum Sauce (page 113)

Sift the flour and baking cocoa into a bowl. Cream the butter and sugar in a mixing bowl until light. Beat in the eggs 1 at a time. Beat in the salt. Add the flour mixture and beat just until blended. Add 1/4 cup cold water and beat until the mixture adheres. Knead the dough on a lightly floured surface and shape into a disc. Chill, wrapped with plastic wrap, for 30 minutes.

Roll the pastry 1/8 inch thick on a lightly floured surface and cut into rounds. Fit the pastry rounds into 20 tartlet pans, removing any excess pastry by rolling the rolling pin over the top.

Preheat a convection oven to 325 degrees. Pierce the pastry with a fork and line with foil and pie weights or dried beans. Bake for 5 minutes. Remove the weights and foil. Bake for 5 minutes longer. Cool on a wire rack.

Beat the chocolate in a heatproof bowl over simmering water. Stir in the warm milk. Beat the whipping cream and yogurt in a mixing bowl until medium peaks form. Soften the gelatin in the 1/3 cup water in a bowl; do not stir.

Add the gelatin mixture to the chocolate mixture and mix well over an ice bath. Fold in the yogurt mixture. Whisk until the mousse begins to thicken. Chill.

To serve, pipe about 2 ounces of the mousse into each tartlet shell and arrange several raspberries stem side down over the mousse. Drizzle 1/4 cup of the Raspberry Sauce onto each dessert plate. Pour the Vanilla Rum Sauce into a squeeze bottle and squeeze a couple of dollops of the sauce on the plate. Create a design using a wooden pick. Arrange the tarts in the center.

Stephanie Campbell
Chef
The Longaberger Company
Dresden, Ohio

Raspberry Sauce
Serves 20

1 pound fresh or frozen raspberries
1/2 cup water

4 ounces sugar
2 tablespoons fresh lemon juice

Combine the raspberries, water, sugar and lemon juice in a saucepan and mix well. Bring to a boil and reduce the heat, stirring occasionally. Simmer for 20 minutes, stirring occasionally. Let stand until cool and process in a food processor or blender until puréed.

Strain the mixture through a fine chinois into a bowl, discarding the solids. For a thicker consistency, pour the strained purée into a clean saucepan and cook until thickened, stirring frequently.

Vanilla Rum Sauce
Makes 2 1/4 cups

6 egg yolks
4 ounces sugar
2 cups heavy cream

1 vanilla bean, split lengthwise
1/4 cup dark rum
1/16 teaspoon salt

Beat the egg yolks and sugar in a mixing bowl until ribbons form. Combine the heavy cream, vanilla bean, rum and salt in a heavy saucepan and mix well. Bring to a boil and remove from the heat. Discard the vanilla bean.

Add some of the hot cream mixture to the egg yolk mixture, stirring constantly. Add the egg yolk mixture to the hot cream mixture and mix well. Cook over low heat until thickened, stirring frequently. Strain into a bowl and chill in an ice bath.

Pecan Tassies

Makes 3 dozen

CREAM CHEESE PASTRY
1 1/2 cups flour
1 1/2 tablespoons sugar
3/4 cup (1 1/2 sticks) butter, softened
4 ounces cream cheese, softened

PECAN FILLING
6 tablespoons chopped pecans
1 1/2 cups packed brown sugar
2 eggs, beaten
2 tablespoons butter, melted

For the crust, mix the flour and sugar in a mixing bowl. Add the butter and cream cheese to the flour mixture and beat just until combined. Divide the pastry into 36 equal portions. Pat each portion over the bottom and up the side of a miniature muffin cup.

For the filling, preheat the oven to 350 degrees. Spoon 1/2 teaspoon of the pecans into each pastry-lined muffin cup.

Whisk the brown sugar, eggs and butter in a bowl until blended. Pour enough of the egg mixture into each prepared muffin cup to fill halfway and sprinkle evenly with the remaining pecans.

Bake for 20 minutes and reduce the oven temperature to 250 degrees. Bake for 15 minutes longer. Cool slightly and remove to a wire rack to cool completely.

Kate has taught at Warren County Career Center since 1997 and is a graduate of the Culinary Institute of America. She recognizes the value of the ProStart® program. She feels ProStart® provides so many fine opportunities for students and will help shape the future of the hospitality industry.

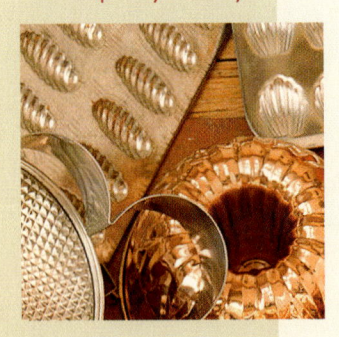

Kate Cole
ProStart® Instructor
Warren County Career Center
Lebanon, Ohio

Lemon Gingersnap Tart
Serves 8

GINGERSNAP CRUST
3 to 4 cups gingersnap cookie crumbs
1/2 to 2/3 cup melted butter

LEMON FILLING
3 cups sweetened condensed milk
6 egg yolks, lightly beaten
1/2 to 3/4 cup lemon juice

For the crust, preheat the oven to 375 degrees. Combine the cookie crumbs and butter in a bowl and mix well. Press the crumb mixture into a 10-inch tart pan and bake for 15 minutes. Reduce the oven temperature to 325 degrees.

For the filling, combine the condensed milk and egg yolks in a bowl and mix well. Add 1/2 cup of the lemon juice and mix well. The filling should begin to thicken. If the filling does not appear thick enough, add the remaining 1/4 cup lemon juice. Spoon the filling over the baked layer and bake for 15 minutes or until set. Let stand until cool.

David Tetzloff
Executive Chef
G. Michael's Bistro
Columbus, Ohio

Danish Puff
Serves 15 to 20

PECAN CRUST
1 cup flour
1/2 cup (1 stick) butter
1/2 cup finely chopped pecans
2 tablespoons water

FILLING
2 cups water
1 cup (2 sticks) butter
2 cups flour
2 teaspoons almond extract
6 eggs

MAPLE ICING
2 cups confectioners' sugar
1/4 cup warm water
1 drop of maple flavoring

For the crust, mix the flour, butter, pecans and water in a bowl until crumbly. Press the crumb mixture to within 1 inch of the sides of a greased 10×15-inch baking pan.

For the filling, preheat the oven to 350 degrees. Bring the water and butter to a boil in a saucepan, stirring occasionally. Add the flour and flavoring and beat until smooth. Add the eggs 1 at a time, beating well after each addition. Spread over the prepared layer and bake for 1 hour.

For the icing, mix the confectioners' sugar, warm water and flavoring in a bowl until of drizzling consistency, adding additional water if needed for the desired consistency. Drizzle the icing over the baked layer and let stand until set. You may add red or green food coloring for a holiday spirit.

Courtney Elliot
Baker
Plaza Inn Restaurant
Mt. Victory, Ohio

Tosca Cups
Makes 15

10 ounces crushed almonds
8 ounces sugar
1 cup (2 sticks) butter, melted
1 1/4 ounces flour
1 3/4 ounces heavy cream
1/16 teaspoon salt

Combine the almonds, sugar, butter, flour, heavy cream and salt in a bowl and mix well. Chill, covered, for 1 hour.

Preheat the oven to 350 degrees. Spoon 2 ounces of the almond mixture 6 inches apart onto a greased baking sheet. Bake for 7 to 10 minutes or until brown. Remove from the oven and cool for 1 minute.

Lift each warm disc with a metal spatula and lay over a teacup to form a cup shape. Let stand until completely cool and remove. Fill the cups with ice cream and hot fudge sauce, or your favorite filling.

Mark Zimmerman
Chef
Spread Eagle Tavern
Hanoverton, Ohio

An *Index* of Contributors

Jonathan Adolph
Guinness Cheesecake, 44
Chocolate Malt Browns, 25
Strada World Cuisine
106 Vine St.
Columbus, OH 43215

John and Kathy Bahas
Coconut Cream Pies, 100
Cookie Pie Pastry, 101
Pecan Pies, 108
Waterloo Restaurant
423 E. Waterloo Rd.
Akron, OH 44319

Johnathan Beck
Vanilla Crème Brûlée, 53
R.J. Snappers Bar & Grill
700 N. High St.
Columbus, OH 43215

Mike Bell
Upside-Down Banana Cream Pie, 98
Pale Ale Caramel Sauce, 99
Candied Pecans, 99
Columbus Brewing Company
525 Short St.
Columbus, OH 43215

Karen Bennett
Raspberry Truffles, 89
Lacentre Conference & Banquet Facilities
25777 Detroit Ave.
Westlake, OH 44145

Debbie Blevins
Red Velvet Cake, 20
Red Velvet Icing, 21
Union Mills Cafectionery
1120 Galena Pike
West Portsmouth, OH 45663

Chef Richard Blondin
Warm Apple Tarts with Rosemary, 111
The Refectory
1092 Bethel Rd.
Columbus, OH 43220

Carli Brant
Torte, 36
Buttercream Icing, 37
Trumbull County JVS
528 Educational Hwy
Warren, OH 44483

Whitney Bray
Chocolate Cake, 10
Chocolate Ganache, 11
Rolled Fondant, 11
Gumpaste Flowers, 11
Northeast Career Center
3871 Stelzer Rd.
Columbus, OH 43220

Stephanie Campbell
Chocolate Tarts with White Chocolate Mousse, 112
Raspberry Sauce, 113
Vanilla Rum Sauce, 113
The Longaberger Company
1500 E. Main St.
Newark, OH 43055

Deane Cobler
Vinegar Pie, 110
Columbus State Community College
550 E. Spring St.
Columbus, OH 43215

Kate Cole
Pecan Tassies, 114
Warren County Career Center
3525 North SR 84
Lebanon, OH 45036

Peter and Laurie Danis
Chocolate Silk Pies, 102
Figlio
1369 Grandview Ave.
Columbus, OH 43212

Denise Denman
Peach Croissant Bread Pudding, 63
Chocolate Fudge Pie, 104
Shaw's Restaurant & Inn
123 N. Broad St.
Lancaster, OH 43130

Andrew Draganski
Coconut Cheesecake with Macadamia Crust, 42
Sixx Asia Bistro
6064 Monroe St.
Sylvania, OH 43560

Merry Draghi
Eggs in Snow, 67
Happy Chicken Farms/Merry Milk Maid
2680 Lewis Centre Way
Urbancrest, OH 43123

Jack Edwards, CEC
Coca-Cola Cake, 12
Coca-Cola Frosting, 13
Raspberry Crème Brûlée, 52
Adams Mark Hotel
50 N. 3rd St.
Columbus, OH 43215

Michael Edwards
Cherry-Strawberry Napoleon, 80
Cherry Strawberry Topping, 81
EHOVE Career Center
316 W. Mason Rd.
Milan, OH 44846

Courtney Elliott
Danish Puff, 116
Plaza Inn Casual Family Restaurant
491 S. Main St., P.O. Box 257
Mt. Victory, OH 43340

Karen Engum
Mandarin Orange Cake, 32
Ohio Hospitality Educational
    Foundation
1525 Bethel Rd., Ste. 301
Columbus, OH 43220

Mary E. Minor Fowler
Pecan Cheesecake, 46
Kettering-Fairmont HS CTC
3301 Shroyer Rd.
Kettering, OH 43140

Steve Frank
Bananas Foster, 76
North High School Akron
985 Gorge Blvd.
Akron, OH 44310

Dewayne C. Gault
Peanut Butter Pie, 107
Invention Family Restaurant
15 Main St. North
Milan, OH 44846

Linda Golden
Deep Dark Chocolate Cake, 16
Tri-Rivers Career Center
2222 Marion-Mt. Gilead Rd.
Marion, OH 43302

Erik Goldstron
Lemon Gratin, 82
Lemon Cream, 83
Cameron's American Bistro
2185 W. Dublin-Granville Rd.
43085

Charles Haas
Honey Kahlúa Semifreddo, 64
Kenmore High School
2140 13th St.
Akron, OH 44314

Kim Hall
Baked Chocolate Mousse, 55
J. Pistone Market
3245 Warrensville Center Rd.
Shaker Hgts., OH 44122

Sheila Hamm
Chocolate Melt Cake, 14
Tri-Rivers Career Center
2222 Marion-Mt. Gilead Rd.
Marion, OH 43302

Jay Haverstick
Lemon Sour Cream Pie, 106
Jay's Restaurant
225 E. Sixth St.
Dayton, OH 45402

Amanda Jones
Apple Pastry, 74
East High School
80 Brittain Rd.
Akron, OH 44308

Kevin Jones
Shark Fin Pie, 109
Mitchell's Fish Market
1245 Olentangy River Rd.
Columbus, OH 43212

Dee Klosterman
Strawberry Pretzel Delight, 88
Klosterman's Derr Road Inn
4343 Derr Rd.
Springfield, OH 45503

Mindy Lacy
Sour Cream Cheesecake, 48
Rooster's Restaurant
Various locations in Columbus, OH

Debbie Lackey
Chocolate Cheesecake, 40
Merry Milk Maid
2680 Lewis Centre Way
Urbancrest, OH 43123

Wayne Leonard
Bread Pudding with Cinnamon
    Sugar Topping, 62
The Golden Jersey Inn at
    Young's Jersey Dairy
6880 Springfield-Xenia Rd.
Yellow Springs, OH 45387

Annette Lieb
French Toast with Date Compote
    and Port Sauce, 79
EHOVE Career Center
316 W. Mason Rd.
Milan, OH 44846

Craig Lomonico
Crème Brûlée, 54
Eastland Career Center
4465 S. Hamilton Rd.
Groveport, OH 43125

Gerry Ludwig, CEC
Caramel Apple Bread Pudding, 60
Gordon Food Service
Various locations in Ohio

Amy Magi
Pumpkin Roll, 33
Phil's Inn Restaurant
1708 E. Perry St.
Port Clinton, OH 43452

Ida Mast
Date Pudding, 65
Brown Bag Apple Pie, 95
Amish Door Restaurant & Village
1210 Winesburg St.,
    P.O. Box 215
Wilmot, OH 44689

Greg Mezey
Orchard to Table Apple Pie, 96
Apple Pie Pastry, 97
Lorain County JVS
15181 SR 58
Oberlin, OH 44074

Tyler K. Mock
Apple Pie with a Squeeze, 92
Cheddar Cheese Pastry, 93
Lorain County JVS
15181 SR 58
Oberlin, OH 44074

John "Bud" Moore II
Bananas Foster, 77
Serenity Tea House
611 Main St.
Coshocton, OH 43812

Lillian Morrison
Texas Sheet Cake, 22
Abner's Country Restaurant
2100 Brice Rd.
Reynoldsburg, OH 43068

Panera Bread
Pear Pecan Crostini, 87
Panera Bread
Various locations in Columbus, OH

Curtis Parker
Apple Walnut Pie, 94
John Q's Steakhouse
55 Public Square
Cleveland, OH 44113

Simon Pesusich
Tiramisù, 70
Zia's Restaurant
20 Main St.
Toledo, OH 43605

Anthony Phenis
Callebaut White Chocolate
    Godiva Mousse, 59
Pier W
12700 Lake Ave.
Lakewood, OH 44107

Dianne Picchino
French Silk Pie, 103
The Clarmont Restaurant
684 S. High St.
Columbus, OH 43215

Carl Quagliata
Lemon Sponge with Raspberry
    Cream Filling, 31
Ristorante Giovanni's
25550 Chagrin Blvd.
Beachwood, OH 44122

Octavio Reyes
Tiramisù, 71
Martini's Italian Bistro
1319 Polaris Pkwy
Columbus, OH 43240

Jeffrey Robinson
Miniature Cheesecakes with
    Lemon Marmalade, 45
Jack's Steakhouse (Marriott)
4277 W. 150th St.
Cleveland, OH 44135

Anthony Romano
Chocolate Mascarpone
    Cheesecake, 41
Players on Madison
14527 Madison
Lakewood, OH 44107

Rob Romph
Bread Pudding, 61
Claire's Winery
7770-7772 W. 150th St.
Middleburg Hgts., OH 44130

Yolanda Sanchez
Toffee Caramel Flan, 66
Tri-Rivers Career Center
2222 Marion-Mt. Gilead Rd.
Marion, OH 43302

Matt Sanders
Chocolate Mousse with
    Raspberry Coulis, 56
Raspberry Coulis, 57
Sugar Cage, 57
EHOVE Career Center
316 W. Mason Rd.
Milan, OH 44846

Sandy Sanders
Praline-Crusted Cheesecake, 47
Ricardo's
4632 Scenic Dr.
Columbus, OH 43214

Ken Schad
Cinnamon-Grilled Pound Cake, 30
Henke Wine
3077 Harrison Ave.
Cincinnati, OH 45211

Jennifer Schiller
German Chocolate Cake, 18
Cream Filling, 19
Coconut Pecan Filling, 19
Springfield-Clark JVS
1901 Selma Rd.
Springfield, OH 45505

Sean Schmidt
Crème Brûlée Cheesecake, 43
Berry Crisp, 85
Parkers Blue Ash Grill
4200 Cooper Rd.
Cincinnai, OH 45242

Rochelle Schrecengost
Apple Dumplings, 75
Trumbull County JVS
528 Educational Hwy
Warren, OH 44483

Asten Singletary
Chocolate Cream Cheese Cake, 24
North High School Akron
985 Gorge Blvd.
Akron, OH 44310

Michelle Spradlin
Piña Colada Party Cakes, 34
Pineapple Frosting, 35
Tri-Rivers Career Center
2222 Marion-Mt. Gilead Rd.
Marion, OH 43302

Jim Taylor
Rhubarb and Strawberry Crisp, 86
Columbus State, Hosp. Mgt. Dept.
550 E. Spring St.
Columbus, OH 43215

David Tetzloff
Panna Cotta, 68
Lemon Gingersnap Tart, 115
G. Michael's Bistro
595 S. Third St.
Columbus, OH 43215

Sara Thomas
Flourless Cakes, 15
Made From Scratch
7500 Montgomery Dr.
Plain City, OH 43064

Anna Mae Tolson
Sweet Potato Cheesecake, 49
Grandview Restaurant
583 E. Main St.
Canfield, OH 44406

Kevin Tucky
Caramel Bananas, 78
Bucks Bar & Grill
192 E. Main St.
Lexington, OH 44904

Artevia Ware
Berry Delicious Cake, 26
White Chocolate Buttercream
    Icing, 27
Madison Comprehensive
    High School
600 Esley Lane
Mansfield, OH 44904

Justin Whites
Chocolate Mousse, 58
Key Lime Pies, 105
Jay's Restaurant
225 E. Sixth St.
Dayton, OH 45402

Jay Williams
Fresh Peach Crisp, 84
Kettering-Fairmont HS CTC
3301 Shroyer Rd.
Kettering, OH 43140

Michelle Willoughby
Warm Chocolate Cake, 23
The Ocean Club
4002 Easton Station
Columbus, OH 43219

Brian Wilson
Carrot Cakes, 28
White Chocolate Frosting, 29
Cap City Diner
1301 Stone Ridge Dr.
Gahanna, OH 43230

Russell Young
Chocolate Espresso Cake, 17
Buttermilk and Coconut Panna
    Cotta, 69
Hyatt on Capital Square
75 East State St.
Columbus, OH 43215

Mark Zimmerman
Tosca Cups, 117
Spread Eagle Tavern
10150 Plymouth St.
Hanoverton, OH 44423

An *Index* of Recipes

A
Almond
    Coconut Cream Pies, 100
    Tosca Cups, 117
Apple
    Apple Dumplings, 75
    Apple Pastry, 74
    Apple Pie with a Squeeze, 92
    Apple Walnut Pie, 94
    Brown Bag Apple Pie, 95
    Caramel Apple Bread Pudding, 60
    Orchard-to-Table Apple Pie, 96
    Warm Apple Tarts with Rosemary, 111
Apple Dumplings, 75
Apple Pastry, 74
Apple Pie Pastry, 97
Apple Pie with a Squeeze, 92
Apple Walnut Pie, 94

B
Baked Chocolate Mousse, 55
Banana
    Bananas Foster, 76
    Bananas Foster for One, 77
    Caramel Bananas, 78
    Upside-Down Banana Cream Pie, 98
Berry. *See also* Raspberry; Strawberry
    Berry Crisp, 85
    Berry Delicious Cake, 26
    Cinnamon-Grilled Pound Cake, 30
Brandied Tiramisù, 70

Bread Puddings
    Bread Pudding, 61
    Bread Pudding with Cinnamon-Sugar Topping, 62
    Caramel Apple Bread Pudding, 60
    Peach Croissant Bread Pudding, 63
Breads. *See also* Bread Puddings
    French Toast with Date Compote and Port Sauce, 79
    Pear Pecan Crostini, 87
Brown Bag Apple Pie, 95
Brownies
    Chocolate Cream Cheese Cake, 24
    Chocolate Malt Brownies, 25
Buttercream Icing, 10, 37
Buttermilk and Coconut Panna Cotta, 69

C
Cakes
    Berry Delicious Cake, 26
    Carrot Cakes, 28
    Chocolate Cake, 10
    Chocolate Cream Cheese Cake, 24
    Chocolate Espresso Cake, 17
    Chocolate Malt Brownies, 25
    Chocolate Melt Cakes, 14
    Cinnamon-Grilled Pound Cake, 30
    Coca-Cola Cake, 12
    Deep Dark Chocolate Cake, 16
    Flourless Cakes, 15
    German Chocolate Cake, 18
    Lemon Sponge with Raspberry Cream Filling, 31
    Mandarin Orange Cake, 32

    Piña Colada Party Cakes, 34
    Pumpkin Roll, 33
    Red Velvet Cake, 20
    Texas Sheet Cake, 22
    Torte, 36
    Warm Chocolate Cake, 23
Callebaut White Chocolate Godiva Mousse, 59
Candied Pecans, 99
Candy
    Raspberry Truffles, 89
Caramel
    Caramel Apple Bread Pudding, 60
    Caramel Bananas, 78
    Pale Ale Caramel Sauce, 99
    Toffee Caramel Flan, 66
Carrot Cakes, 28
Cheddar Cheese Pastry, 93
Cheese. *See also* Cream Cheese; Mascarpone Cheese
    Cheddar Cheese Pastry, 93
    Pear Pecan Crostini, 87
Cheesecakes
    Chocolate Cheesecake, 40
    Chocolate Mascarpone Cheesecake, 41
    Coconut Cheesecake with Macadamia Crust, 42
    Crème Brûlée Cheesecake, 43
    Guinness Cheesecake, 44
    Miniature Cheesecakes with Lemon Marmalade, 45
    Pecan Cheesecake, 46
    Praline-Crusted Cheesecake, 47
    Sour Cream Cheesecake, 48
    Sweet Potato Cheesecake, 49

Cherry
   Cherry Strawberry Napoleon, 80
   Cherry Strawberry Topping, 81
   Date Compote, 79
   French Toast with Date Compote and Port Sauce, 79

Chocolate. *See also* White Chocolate
   Baked Chocolate Mousse, 55
   Chocolate Buttercream Icing, 18
   Chocolate Cake, 10
   Chocolate Cheesecake, 40
   Chocolate Cookie Crumb Crust, 109
   Chocolate Cream Cheese Cake, 24
   Chocolate Espresso Cake, 17
   Chocolate Fudge Pie, 104
   Chocolate Ganache, 11
   Chocolate Graham Cracker Crust, 41
   Chocolate Malt Brownies, 25
   Chocolate Mascarpone Cheesecake, 41
   Chocolate Melt Cakes, 14
   Chocolate Mousse, 58
   Chocolate Mousse with Raspberry Coulis, 56
   Chocolate Nut Frosting, 22
   Chocolate Pudding Icing, 36
   Chocolate Sauce, 25
   Chocolate Silk Pies, 102
   Chocolate Tarts with White Chocolate Mousse, 112
   Coca-Cola Cake, 12
   Coca-Cola Frosting, 13
   Deep Dark Chocolate Cake, 16
   Flourless Cakes, 15
   French Silk Pie, 103
   German Chocolate Cake, 18
   One-Bowl Chocolate Buttercream Frosting, 16
   Pecan Cheesecake, 46
   Raspberry Truffles, 89
   Red Velvet Cake, 20
   Shark Fin Pie, 109
   Texas Sheet Cake, 22
   Tiramisù, 71
   Torte, 36
   Warm Chocolate Cake, 23

Chocolate Cake, 10
Chocolate Cheesecake, 40
Chocolate Cream Cheese Cake, 24
Chocolate Espresso Cake, 17
Chocolate Fudge Pie, 104
Chocolate Ganache, 11
Chocolate Malt Brownies, 25
Chocolate Mascarpone Cheesecake, 41
Chocolate Melt Cakes, 14
Chocolate Mousse, 58
Chocolate Mousse with Raspberry Coulis, 56
Chocolate Silk Pies, 102
Chocolate Tarts with White Chocolate Mousse, 112
Cinnamon-Grilled Pound Cake, 30
Coca-Cola Cake, 12
Coca-Cola Frosting, 13

Coconut
   Buttermilk and Coconut Panna Cotta, 69
   Coconut Cheesecake with Macadamia Crust, 42
   Coconut Cream Pies, 100
   Coconut Pecan Filling, 19
   Piña Colada Party Cakes, 34

Coffee
   Brandied Tiramisù, 70
   Chocolate Espresso Cake, 17
   Honey Kahlúa Semifreddo, 64
   Tiramisù, 71

Cookie Pie Pastries, 101

Cream Cheese
   Chocolate Cream Cheese Cake, 24
   Chocolate Mascarpone Cheesecake, 41
   Coconut Cheesecake with Macadamia Crust, 42
   Crème Brûlée Cheesecake, 43
   Cream Cheese Filling, 33
   Cream Cheese Pastry, 114
   Guinness Cheesecake, 44
   Honey Kahlúa Semifreddo, 64
   Lemon Gratin, 82
   Miniature Cheesecakes with Lemon Marmalade, 45
   Peanut Butter Pie, 107
   Pecan Cheesecake, 46
   Praline-Crusted Cheesecake, 47
   Sour Cream Cheesecake, 48
   Strawberry Pretzel Delight, 88
   Sweet Potato Cheesecake, 49
   White Chocolate Buttercream Icing, 27
   White Chocolate Frosting, 29

Crème Brûlée
  Crème Brûlée, 54
  Crème Brûlée Cheesecake, 43
  Raspberry Crème Brûlée, 52
  Vanilla Crème Brûlée, 53
Cream Filling, 19
Crisps
  Berry Crisp, 85
  Fresh Peach Crisp, 84
  Rhubarb and Strawberry Crisp, 86
Crusts. See also Pastry
  Chocolate Cookie Crumb Crust, 109
  Chocolate Graham Cracker Crust, 41
  Gingersnap Crust, 115
  Graham Cracker Crust, 48, 98, 105
  Macadamia Crust, 42
  Pecan Crust, 46, 102, 116
  Praline Crust, 47
  Pretzel Crust, 88
  Vanilla Wafer Crust, 44, 45, 49
Custards. See Bread Puddings; Crème Brûlée; Panna Cotta; Puddings; Tiramisù

D
Danish Puff, 116
Date
  Date Pudding, 65
  French Toast with Date Compote and Port Sauce, 79
Decorations
  Candied Pecans, 99
  Gumpaste Flowers, 11
  Sugar Cages, 57
  Sugared Orange Zest, 81
Deep Dark Chocolate Cake, 16

E
Eggs in Snow, 67

F
Fillings
  Chocolate Ganache, 11
  Coconut Pecan Filling, 19
  Cream Cheese Filling, 33
  Cream Filling, 19
  Raspberry Cream Filling, 31
  Raspberry Filling, 37
Flourless Cakes, 15
French Silk Pie, 103
French Toast with Date Compote and Port Sauce, 79
Fresh Peach Crisp, 84
Frostings/Icings
  Buttercream Icing, 10, 37
  Chocolate Buttercream Icing, 18
  Chocolate Nut Frosting, 22
  Chocolate Pudding Icing, 36
  Coca-Cola Frosting, 13
  Maple Icing, 116
  One-Bowl Chocolate Buttercream Frosting, 16
  Pineapple Frosting, 32, 35
  Red Velvet Icing, 21
  Rolled Fondant, 11
  Vanilla Pudding Icing, 36
  White Chocolate Buttercream Icing, 27
  White Chocolate Frosting, 29
Fruit Desserts. See Apple; Banana; Cherry; Date; Lemon; Lime; Orange; Peach; Pineapple; Raspberry; Strawberry

G
German Chocolate Cake, 18
Guinness Cheesecake, 44
Gumpaste Flowers, 11

H
Honey Kahlùa Semifreddo, 64

K
Key Lime Pies, 105

L
Lemon
  Lemon Cream, 83
  Lemon Gingersnap Tart, 115
  Lemon Gratin, 82
  Lemon Marmalade, 45
  Lemon Sour Cream Pie, 106
  Lemon Sponge with Raspberry Cream Filling, 31
  Miniature Cheesecakes with Lemon Marmalade, 45
Lime
  Key Lime Pies, 105

M
Macadamia
  Coconut Cheesecake with Macadamia Crust, 42
  Macadamia Crust, 42
Mandarin Orange Cake, 32
Mascarpone Cheese
  Brandied Tiramisù, 70
  Chocolate Mascarpone Cheesecake, 41
  Tiramisù, 71
  Miniature Cheesecakes with Lemon Marmalade, 45

Mousse
    Baked Chocolate Mousse, 55
    Callebaut White Chocolate Godiva Mousse, 59
    Chocolate Mousse, 58
    Chocolate Mousse with Raspberry Coulis, 56

N
Nuts. *See* Almond; Macadamia; Pecan; Walnut

O
Orange
    Mandarin Orange Cake, 32
    Sugared Orange Zest, 81
Orchard-to-Table Apple Pie, 96

P
Pale Ale Caramel Sauce, 99
Panna Cotta
    Buttermilk and Coconut Panna Cotta, 69
    Panna Cotta, 68
Pastry, 94. *See also* Crusts
    Apple Pastry, 74
    Apple Pie Pastry, 97
    Cheddar Cheese Pastry, 93
    Cookie Pie Pastries, 101
    Cream Cheese Pastry, 114
    Danish Puff, 116
    Tosca Cups, 117
    Vinegar Pie Pastry, 110
Peach
    Fresh Peach Crisp, 84
    Peach Brandy Sauce, 63
    Peach Croissant Bread Pudding, 63

Peanut Butter
    Peanut Butter Pie, 107
    Shark Fin Pie, 109
Pear Pecan Crostini, 87
Pecan
    Candied Pecans, 99
    Chocolate Nut Frosting, 22
    Chocolate Silk Pies, 102
    Coca-Cola Frosting, 13
    Coconut Pecan Filling, 19
    Pear Pecan Crostini, 87
    Pecan Cheesecake, 46
    Pecan Crust, 46, 102, 116
    Pecan Pies, 108
    Pecan Tassies, 114
Pecan Cheesecake, 46
Pecan Pies, 108
Pecan Tassies, 114
Pies. *See also* Tarts
    Apple Pie with a Squeeze, 92
    Apple Walnut Pie, 94
    Brown Bag Apple Pie, 95
    Chocolate Fudge Pie, 104
    Chocolate Silk Pies, 102
    Coconut Cream Pies, 100
    French Silk Pie, 103
    Key Lime Pies, 105
    Lemon Sour Cream Pie, 106
    Orchard-to-Table Apple Pie, 96
    Peanut Butter Pie, 107
    Pecan Pies, 108
    Shark Fin Pie, 109
    Upside-Down Banana Cream Pie, 98
    Vinegar Pie, 110
Piña Colada Party Cakes, 34

Pineapple
    Buttermilk and Coconut Panna Cotta, 69
    Carrot Cakes, 28
    Piña Colada Party Cakes, 34
    Pineapple Frosting, 32, 35
    Praline-Crusted Cheesecake, 47
Puddings
    Date Pudding, 65
    Eggs in Snow, 67
    Honey Kahlúa Semifreddo, 64
    Toffee Caramel Flan, 66
Pumpkin Roll, 33

R
Raspberry
    Chocolate Mousse with Raspberry Coulis, 56
    Chocolate Tarts with White Chocolate Mousse, 112
    Lemon Gratin, 82
    Lemon Sponge with Raspberry Cream Filling, 31
    Raspberry Coulis, 56
    Raspberry Cream Filling, 31
    Raspberry Crème Brûlée, 52
    Raspberry Filling, 37
    Raspberry Sauce, 113
    Raspberry Truffles, 89
    Torte, 36
Raspberry Coulis, 56
Raspberry Crème Brûlée, 52
Raspberry Filling, 37
Raspberry Sauce, 113
Raspberry Truffles, 89
Red Velvet Cake, 20
Red Velvet Icing, 21
Rhubarb and Strawberry Crisp, 86
Rolled Fondant, 11

S

Sauces
- Brown Sugar Sauce, 65
- Chocolate Sauce, 25
- Lemon Cream, 83
- Lemon Marmalade, 45
- Pale Ale Caramel Sauce, 99
- Peach Brandy Sauce, 63
- Raspberry Coulis, 56
- Raspberry Sauce, 113
- Vanilla Rum Sauce, 113

Shark Fin Pie, 109
Sour Cream Cheesecake, 48

Strawberry
- Cherry Strawberry Napoleon, 80
- Cherry Strawberry Topping, 81
- Crème Brûlée Cheesecake, 43
- Rhubarb and Strawberry Crisp, 86
- Strawberry Pretzel Delight, 88
- Strawberry Topping, 88

Sugar Cages, 57
Sugared Orange Zest, 81
Sweet Potato Cheesecake, 49

T

Tarts
- Chocolate Tarts with White Chocolate Mousse, 112
- Lemon Gingersnap Tart, 115
- Pecan Tassies, 114
- Warm Apple Tarts with Rosemary, 111

Texas Sheet Cake, 22

Tiramisù, 71
- Brandied Tiramisù, 70

Toffee Caramel Flan, 66

Toppings
- Cherry Strawberry Topping, 81
- Cinnamon-Sugar Topping, 62
- Oat Topping, 85
- Sour Cream Topping, 47, 48
- Strawberry Topping, 88
- Walnut Topping, 94

Torte, 36
Tosca Cups, 117

U

Upside-Down Banana Cream Pie, 98

V

Vanilla Crème Brûlée, 53
Vanilla Rum Sauce, 113
Vinegar Pie, 110

W

Walnut
- Apple Pastry, 74
- Apple Walnut Pie, 94
- Bread Pudding, 61
- Caramel Bananas, 78
- Coconut Cream Pies, 100
- Date Pudding, 65
- Walnut Topping, 94
- Warm Apple Tarts with Rosemary, 111

Warm Chocolate Cake, 23

White Chocolate
- Berry Delicious Cake, 26
- Callebaut White Chocolate Godiva Mousse, 59
- Chocolate Tarts with White Chocolate Mousse, 112
- White Chocolate Buttercream Icing, 27
- White Chocolate Frosting, 29

DESSERT
First

Ohio Hospitality Educational Foundation
1525 Bethel Road, Suite 301
Columbus, Ohio 43220
614-442-9374
www.ohef.com

Name _____

Street Address _____

City _____ State _____ Zip _____

Telephone _____ Email _____

YOUR ORDER	QUANTITY	TOTAL
Dessert First at $12.95 per book		$
Postage, handling, and sales tax at $6.50 per book		$
	TOTAL	$

Method of Payment: [ ] American Express   [ ] Discover   [ ] MasterCard   [ ] Visa
[ ] Check enclosed payable to Ohio Hospitality Educational Foundation

Account Number _____ Expiration Date _____

Cardholder Name _____

Signature _____

Photocopies will be accepted.